THE RAGDOLL
and THE MARINE

A Memoir

NICOLE A. CALVO

THE RAGDOLL and THE MARINE
Copyright © 2016 Nicole A. Calvo

www.nicolecalvo.com

Formatted by The Book Khaleesi
Cover Photo by Forrest C. Fujikawa
ISBN: 978-0-692-94104-1

Table of Contents

To My Mother,

Natividad "Natty" R.C. Calvo

~ and ~

In Memory

Of Our Marine Liberator,

Richard Washburn

Foreword

It was a little over two years ago when Nicole first shared bits of her mother's life story with me. The fascinating details of her mom's life triggered my initial suggestion to turn these memories into a book. After some steady persuasion, Nicole agreed and started chapter one of what would end up being one of the most memorable true stories I've ever read. I laughed, I cried, and I finished the book feeling like a better person.

The Ragdoll and The Marine is a wonderful story which I have read three times to date. Each time taking away something more than the time before. Nicole is a truly talented writer with the ability to tell a story that will fill your imagination with exciting images and fill your heart with emotion.

I love this book! I'm extremely proud of Nicole and the finished product!

– JOHN HUGULEY
Writer/Photographer

Chapter One

THE GIFT

Each Christmas, like a typical child, I vividly remember looking under my family's festive holiday tree for my gifts. However, unlike most kids, I longed for and waited patiently to receive a perfect package in particular. Even though I may have had three or four gifts, nothing could compare with the specific, special and spectacular one. Frantically searching for my name on the gift tags before anyone caught me rummaging under the Christmas tree, I would pull out the boxes or bags that were properly labeled: "To Nicci, From Santa", and instantly know from its size and weight as I excitedly shook it, that once again, I did not receive it. Being a perpetual optimist, the next year, as in the years preceding, I would pray to Jesus, plead with Santa and wish upon a star for the one gift that every good, little girl wanted to own, play with and look like when all grown up...Barbie!

As a young and impressionable child, Barbie was for me, more than just a toy, she was the very essence of beauty and poise. She was an adult, who did what all adults do-whatever they want! She was a trend-setter, the envy of the popular crowd, and most importantly was allowed to have a boyfriend! This doll was so special that everyone around me seemed to have, not just one, but a slew of them. I even had a male cousin who owned a Barbie, even though we were only allowed to play with her when no one was around and with the bedroom door locked. He told me that she was a spy, like a female James Bond, and I was sworn to secrecy! I just

THE RAGDOLL and THE MARINE

wanted one; even if I could borrow her from my best friend, for one day. This would have satisfied me and I would have been a happy and blissful child. Barbie was and had everything that I could not and did not have!

Strangely, my fixation with this iconic toy stemmed from my mother. Not that she had a fascination for this slice of Americana, or wanted me to emulate the most perfect female ever, rather, because she was obsessed with another kind of toy- a rag doll. For Natty, a Raggedy Ann doll was far more intriguing than the blond plastic bombshell with interchangeable outfits, a sports car, a house in Malibu and, let's not forget, the perfect male counterpart – Ken. Hence, I grew up, never owning a Barbie but envious of all my childhood friends and family members that had her in their possession. Of course, my collection of rag dolls from my mother's generous gift-giving over the years could rival even the most avid doll collector in the country.

At the time, I detested the very sight of any toy that was made from stitching, stuffing and fabric. It was hard for me to believe that my mother had the best of intentions each time I received for Christmas or my birthday another stuffed doll. I was convinced that I was an adopted child whom she did not really care for or that somehow a store clerk who sold Mom the toy, accidentally put the wrong doll in the gift box and wrapped it up. So by chance, she never quite gave me what I really wanted. It was easier to make believe that these versions of the facts were true than to admit to myself that Mom just loved rag dolls.

Although some people may think that my Mom's fetish, for the red-head with the country, hick get-up, was because of the doll's simplistic, modest and wholesome image. Thereby this raggedy girl and her raggedy brother would serve as good role models for my sisters and me to mimic, so that we would grow-up to become self-less, natural and morally up-standing women. In theory, this made a lot of sense to me as an adult, but nothing was further from the truth…Mom's fascination and adoration of rag dolls was because her earliest memory as a child, of something good, safe and peaceful was the direct result of a simple gesture of kindness from, of all people, a lean, mean, fighting Marine!

When someone references the old adage, "Education begins at home" or "A child's first teacher is their parent", these words of wisdom always rang true for my siblings and me, because Mom was the one who introduced us to the wonderful world of reading as she recited Mother Goose nursery rhymes to us, sang and danced with us, and last but certainly not least, told the best make-believe stories, which always kept us on the edge of our seats. She was a stay-at- home mother with six children and until we reached the age to enter kindergarten, she was the greatest teacher ever, which probably explains why four out of six of her children became educators.

Eventually we would all be off to school but fondly, I remember that she would sometimes encourage us to stay home on the weekdays to once again be enrolled in "Mommy School". Her love for story-telling, coupled with her animated voice and expressive facial gestures, are perhaps the main reasons it was so difficult for us to realize and believe that the story of how she came to be the recipient of a rag doll from a soldier was true! We thought, or at least I thought, that she made the whole thing up. Like most of her other stories, it had all the elements of excitement, terror and resolution that all great tales require.

She would tell us that our tiny island of Guam was invaded by the Japanese Imperial Army and that after a few years of this foreign occupation, our people were liberated by United States Marines in World War II. But somehow, I just could not grasp in my perfect little world, that Guam, my peaceful island home and paradise, became the backdrop for violence and fear. Nor could I fathom that a little, four-year-old girl born on December 26, 1939, and appropriately named Natividad, in honor of the feast of the Nativity of Christ, was an innocent witness to all the horrors and atrocities of war.

Chapter Two

THE KINDNESS OF STRANGERS

I was scared!" This was what I remembered my mom always stressing to us as she recounted her story about her beloved rag doll. Perhaps this is what made me think that she made the whole story up, because as a child I couldn't understand why a little girl would be afraid to receive a toy. Of course, in hindsight, she was almost two years old when her island home was invaded by the Japanese on December 8, 1941, and lived the next three years of her very young life directly in the throes of the War in the Pacific.

THE RAGDOLL and THE MARINE

For Natty, the memory of the war, understandably, would bring back feelings of fear and sadness. Although, she did not recall specific incidents that would cause such despairing emotions, there were however, certain images or sites that would trigger a flashback of her war experience. For instance, as an adult, I would drive mom to run errands or go shopping around Guam and whenever she would see an outcropping of palm trees against a savannah like grassland, she would often tell me that the "Oasis" (As she would refer to it) of trees somehow made her instantly become absolutely quiet inside. It would make her think of something sad, depressing and lonely.

"I think it reminds me of the War, but I don't know why?" was often her explanation for such a raw reaction to something so seemingly harmless and non-threatening.

I never said a word to her as she would tell me these bits of memory recall but I would often think about the power of the human mind. Its ability to block disturbing thoughts, so that in the face of it one becomes in denial or is able to cope with such a harsh reality or frightening truth, is remarkable. At the time, I reasoned that Mom's forlorn feeling, as she passed these unconscious remnants of her past, was because her four-year old little brain was too young and immature to hold on to such tragic events, thankfully and rightfully so. It was not too long before her memory was flooded with the facts. She would soon discover and recognize why these trees were so significant and made such a lasting impression on her reverie.

Somehow, Mom's story of the war always began at the end of the occupation by the invading forces.

"A day before Guam was liberated, Grandma gave birth to my baby sister Carmen, in a concentration camp that we were all forced to march to by the Japanese soldiers. Imagine how strong she must've been to give birth to a child in such an awful place. My brothers and sisters would tease your Auntie Carmen that the reason she is so dark is because she was born in the dirt and mud of Manenggon." Natty would jokingly tell us.

She proceeded to explain that prior to the recapture of Guam by the U.S. Army and Marines Corps, the Americans had been bombing the tiny island for nearly two weeks in July of 1944, before its eventual liberation on the 21st of the month. Subsequently, the Chamorro people were told to walk to a remote area in the southeastern end of the island that would serve as a concentration camp for the locals to keep them from revolting against their Japanese occupiers or giving away locations of their fortifications to the American forces that waited patiently on battleships a few miles away from the island as their artillery were heavily engaged.

"I remember seeing people vomiting everywhere and using the bathroom on themselves, as we were walking to the camp and I felt sick from the smell and sight of it." Mom relayed this fact to us with such expression in her voice, hand gestures and face that one could wholly visualize the horrific scene. This part of her story always made one of my siblings' squeal, "EEEWWW, that's so gross Mom!"

Then she would say, "This sickness is what people call Dysentery, and many Chamorro, including my baby brother, died of it after the war. You see we didn't have a hospital or clinic that we could go to, to get better."

Natty continued to explain how people would contract the illness and how sad it was that although her little brother lived through the liberation, his little body could not survive this painful disease. The sorrow in her eyes, when she relived this tragic loss, was clearly evident even as she did her best to mask the hurt.

Courageously she would continue, "I remember that there were only a few soldiers surrounding the camp but people kept whispering about rumors that the Japanese were going to kill all of us. Then the night my mother gave birth to my baby sister, my oldest brother Herman snuck out of the camp only to return early the next morning to tell my mother and father that the Americans had landed on the island and were fighting the Japanese in Asan. My father looked at my mother and we knew that Uncle Sam had returned to us."

Prior to the World War II invasion, the United States had acquired Guam in 1898, as a spoil of war from the Spanish Crown. For nearly 40 years, the Chamorro were a people with no U.S. Citizenry but nonetheless, had a fierce loyalty to America. The island was under the supervision of the Department of the Navy, with its commanding officer serving as the Governor of Guam, to maintain order in the most western territory of the United States. During the Japanese occupation, what few Marines and Navy personnel as well as the Caucasian civilians who lived on the island were imprisoned and transferred by ship to a POW camp in Japan. Later as an act of defiance and a show of faithfulness, a few locals composed a catchy jingle that proved their undying hope and continuous allegiance for the Stars and Stripes to one day return to Guam.

Mom would sing the refrain while nodding her head left to right, "Mister Sam, Sam, My dear Uncle Sam, won't you please come back to Guam!" This was the only part of the song that she remembered but it served its purpose as she continued with her fascinating story about war-torn Guam.

"Mommy, tell us about when you got the dolly from the soldier?" one of us would insist of her.

"Well, this is what I remember. We were allowed to return to our village homes after the American soldiers liberated us from the camp. So one day, I was walking with Grandma down one of the dusty roads and it must've been early in the morning because there weren't many people out. I don't recall

THE RAGDOLL and THE MARINE

where we were going or coming from but suddenly I saw trucks and jeeps and lots of soldiers heading toward us. Some Chamorro said that the Americans were giving people chocolate or canned goods, so I was excited to see these white men because they were nice and smiled, not like the Japanese soldiers before. But then all of a sudden, one soldier came toward me and my mom, and I remember being scared! I don't know why I was afraid maybe it was because he was the first white man that I saw up close and he seemed as tall as a giant. His hair was almost as white as his skin and he had eyes the color of the ocean, which no one in Guam had, at least no one that I remembered when I was little. He was looking straight at us and was holding something in his hands. I thought he was going to hurt us but the next thing I knew, he bent down and held out his hand with whatever he was clutching. It was a rag doll. I had never seen anything like it before but I don't think I wanted to take it at first. It was like I was afraid that my mother wouldn't allow me to take something from a complete stranger. But that wasn't the case, because the next thing I remember I was holding my very first toy in my hands. I knew right at that moment that he and the doll were good and safe, and I was no longer scared! And that was it, we walked away from the soldier and I never saw him again. But I'll never forget that day or that Marine! It was the kindest thing that anyone had ever done for me!"

This was the way my mother recapped this tragic story as we sat listening to her eager with anticipation and fear. She always ended it on a positive note.

Chapter Three

SENSORY OVERLOAD

It's funny how little things have a way of jogging the memory! The smell of chicken frying in a vat of oil, I always associate with my Grandmother. Perhaps because no one could make fried chicken as good as Grandma Chalan Pago did. She seemed to always be cooking her famous chicken whenever Mom would take us to visit her. Any song from Prince's Purple Rain album, reminds me of California. I suppose it was the summer blockbuster hit that I happen to watch, when we were on a family vacation. The sight of a small paper Dixie cup, it never fails but I nauseatingly correlate it with "Swish", that bluish-green fluoride that we had to take in elementary school. What was probably a 30-second time frame seemed to be hours when that disgusting liquid was in your mouth, and being forewarned by your teachers not to swallow it never helped to ease that torturous process. Of course, some of these little things produce nice, warm and fuzzy feelings while others provoke the complete opposite, but one thing is for sure it inundates our memory at the sheer sight, sound or smell of it!

Unfortunately, sometimes memory recall requires another trick of the mind – retracing your steps! Where did I put my car keys? Start at the beginning, where did I go or come from and recount the steps taken to this point. Very soon, I'm walking back to the kitchen sink as I recall placing my keys on the windowsill before I started to wash the dishes. Most of the time a combination of both techniques to recollect the past, works like a charm, as was the case for Natty.

Evidently, the oasis of palm trees flooded her memory but the specifics of why or what happened to make her think of the war whenever she saw them was still a mystery! The only way that she was able to recognize and understand her associating these trees with the war, was to retrace or rather relive her march to Manenggon, the concentration camp that many Chamorro were forced to walk to before their subsequent liberation by American Forces.

The 21st of July marks the official day of the liberation of the Island and her people by U.S. Armed Forces from the invading Japanese Imperial Army in 1944. This local holiday holds as much pomp, pageantry and patriotism in Guam as the Fourth of July does for the United States. Each summer, there are numerous tributes and celebrations organized throughout the island: carnival grounds are erected for people to enjoy; a parade of floats and military marching units on the actual Liberation Day is held along Marine Corps Drive in the capital, Hagatna with throngs of island residents along both sides of the main thoroughfare cheering and waving; and the general well-wishes of peace and tranquility of a modern Guam are encouraged and enjoyed by all residents and visitors alike.

On the occasion of the 60th Anniversary of the Liberation of Guam, a non-profit organization whose founding members were victims of the infamous concentration camp, organized a commemorative march back to the Manenggon site. It was the first time Chamorro survivors, their families and the general public were able to revisit this treacherous location in Guam's history. This was an opportunity that Natty felt very strongly about participating in and so I was obliged to accompany her on this journey back to a place that she had spoken about in the past with such poignancy and pain.

I took the liberty of inviting two of my girl-friends to join Mom and me as we attended the

THE RAGDOLL and THE MARINE

March. Fortunately for us, Glenda's grandfather, Tun Juan Pangelinan, also wanted to participate as he was a survivor of the camp and a young man in his twenties when the Japanese occupation occurred. His memory was obviously much sharper than Mom's as he told us of what the conditions were like in July of 1944, when the majority of the people were forced to walk to this valley in the eastern end of the island while Japanese soldiers with bayonets flanked the long line of Chamorro filing into the narrow pathway. They would use their knives affixed to guns to ensure that the old, young and weak would not slow down or fall out of line. He described the torrential rains that month which made the trek even more treacherous and slippery as for some reason the heavy downpour seemed harsher, colder and crueler as many were ordered to walk into this dense jungle area with no shelter or food when they arrived at their destination. He essentially said it was a women and children's march because most of the men were ordered to help clear a landing airstrip in a village north of Manenggon. The men would only be able to join their wives, mothers and children late at night after working long hours clearing the runway. His account of the ingenuity of the people was what struck a chord with me; instead of feeling helpless and depressed, the Chamorro people used whatever natural materials they could to construct makeshift shelters and bedding for their families. Tun Juan's detailed descriptions continued as we began with what seemed a very emotional walk on a now paved road that led into the notorious site.

This revisit was special, not because of the high-ranking government officials in attendance or the amount of media coverage it received or even the hundreds of people who were present but because among the crowd, one could see the elders who were obviously much younger and more nimble at the time of the war, now walking back to Manenggon with canes, wheel chairs, or walkers but determined to make it. There must have been less than a hundred of them, but their presence made this memorial march so powerful and profound. People walked with a quietness and respect that was palpable, and these elders, with such frail bodies, seemed like giants among the rest of us who only heard their stories, and were born and lived in a different time.

As we walked along the surfaced street, the sound of the river that ran adjacent to it, was eerily peaceful even with the rainy season in July in Guam which made the fresh water swollen and engorged. Prepared for a heavy downpour that would not be unusual at this time of year in our tropical paradise, we walked with our umbrellas in hand, but the sun appeared in all its glory over the cortege of attendants. This was not the weather that the survivors recalled enduring those 60 years earlier. There was a short bridge half way through the march and from that vantage point Natty began to shout, "Nicci, there are the trees! I remember now why it always made me feel sad and scared! NOW, I remember!"

At first, I thought my mother was losing her mind and looked around the crowd as if to beg forgiveness for her outburst but then, I looked at Natty and saw the tears welling up in her eyes and I knew instantly that she was experiencing a total memory recall, it was evident from her heart-rending facial expression.

"Mom, are you okay?" I nervously pleaded with her.

"Yes, my baby, I remember it like it was yesterday. My father was holding me on his shoulders as we walked with all the other people into the valley. I must've been looking at those palm trees along the edge of the river heading into the camp. He looked up at me and I knew that he was scared but I didn't know why."

She made a sweeping gesture and continued, "My mother's belly was so large from being pregnant that she was holding my baby brother on her hips while my father held on to her other hand to guide her through the slippery trail. I could hear people sobbing and moaning but everyone kept moving. We were scared that the soldiers would hit us with their guns, so we just walked with our heads down but as quickly as we could. Oh gosh I remember everything now! "

Her memory was now fully restored, but I was not sure that this was a good thing for Mom. I was regretting our participation in this historic event as I began to doubt the outcome and impact it would have on her. What if she went into a depression because of it? How would she be able to cope with this unspeakable reality that she could no longer hide in the caverns of her mind? Would this horrific experience scar her irreparably? How could I help her overcome this trauma?

I was frightened for Natty but more so, I was frightened for me. Mom was always strong of mind, body and heart. She was our rock when we lost our father from a heart-attack at the age of 44. Left with six children to raise, she, who was a 42-year-old housewife with no work experience, seemed to have an inner strength and resiliency that oozed out of her right when we needed her most. But like most people, there is a breaking point and I was not sure if this experience had made her reach it.

With the biggest smile on her face, she looked up toward the sky and said, "Oh my Father in Heaven, thank you for making the Americans come to save us. We would've all been killed if they came one day later, I'm certain of it!"

Her response, in the midst of my self-doubt, made me realize that Natty was also strong in spirit. This unshakeable and hope-filled faith of hers was perhaps the single most profound trait that she possessed which made her will to live and thrive, and not merely survive, in life.

Chapter Four

QUESTIONS

I sometimes look at other people's kids and wonder what I was like when I was a child. All the stereotypes of personalities come to mind: the brainy child, always reading and pulling straight A's in school, that wasn't me. The gifted child, those who are artistically or musically inclined, again not me. The athletic/outdoorsy child those whose favorite pastimes include running, playing ball of any size or type, and swimming, activities that were all foreign to me. Neither was I the rebellious child or the loner. I want to believe that as a child I was the curious and precocious one.

The reason was simply because, after Natty told her war story, I always had a ton of questions that I wanted to ask: *what did your doll look like, what was a soldier doing with a rag-doll in the middle the war anyway, were other kids getting toys from the marines too and lastly, what do you think happened to the soldier after the war?* But the day I sat in our kitchen table while my mom was washing dishes and I asked, "Whatever happened to that doll", was the moment I realized that some things are better left unknown.

If there was one thing about Natty that you could count on, it would be her happy, positive disposition. So, there was never a moment that I felt like I couldn't or shouldn't ask or tell her anything. You knew instantly as you looked at her that the single most significant facial feature that stood out against all others, where she was concerned, was her smile. She literally could light-up a room with it and once her lips curled up, her very pronounced cheekbones would get even higher and fuller. So, her reaction at first to my question was confusing. She looked straight forward and immediately her big brown eyes turned glassy while she beamed from ear to ear. She seemed so animated and full of joy at that very moment but her answer shocked me.

"Grandma took the doll from me and burned it", she said.

I could hear the pain in her voice and instantly I wished I never asked that question. It was obvious that whatever happened to make my grandmother take her five-year-old daughter's toy and destroy it, was a terribly traumatizing ordeal for my mother. But true to form, Natty made her peace with it and said, "I actually blocked this memory of my doll burning in a fire pit for over 20 years."

"What do you mean Mom? Why'd Grandma do it?" I knew I shouldn't have pressed her for the details but I had a difficult time trying to understand how my loving and affectionate grandmother that I grew up adoring, could be so cruel to an innocent child.

She continued staring out the kitchen window as if in a trance and proceeded to explain, "I don't remember where or what the occasion was but Grandma was with some of her elderly friends. I must've been nearly 30 by then and as I walked in the room I overheard her tell them that after the war she washed uniforms for many of the marine soldiers to earn some cash. I always loved listening to stories about the war so I went over to sit by them and then she pointed to me and said, 'My daughter Natty here, was given a rag-doll by one of the soldiers in the 3rd Marine Division. She carried that doll with her wherever she went and never let it out of her sight. That's why I had to take it away from her; it was filthy!'"

I was staring at Natty and she became very still and quiet. I wanted to say something to her, to break this awkward silence that seemed to last forever, but for the first time in my life, I was afraid of how she would respond. I could see that the memory of her doll being torn away from her was still hurtful as her voice cracked when she finally spoke again. This time, she no longer had a smile on her face.

"I sat there listening to my mother recount her story after the war, and I remember that very day. It was beautiful and sunny. My cousins and I were running around the yard and I was holding my doll. And one of them asked me to hold the doll and I said 'no'. My dolly was so special to me. If I knew then that I could wash and clean her, to stop my mom from taking her, I would've!"

Natty proceeded to explain that as the sun was setting, my grandmother came up to her and said in our native tongue:

"Natty, haga-hu, nae-yu i moneka!"/ "Natty, my daughter, give me the doll!"

But Natty refused and started walking away from her quickly as she squeezed tightly to the doll, holding it closely to her chest. My grandmother followed after her and continued to plead with Natty to give her the dirty rag doll. But the more she persisted, the more adamantly Natty refused her, "Mungga Nana-hu pot fabot!"/ "No Mommy, please!"

Tears rolled off her cheeks as she explained how her mother gently held her in place, squatted down toward her and pried the tightly held doll from her arms. She turned to face me with a distant look in her eyes and I knew that this memory was just as painful to her as the march to the concentration camp.

Gently she whispered, "That doll was the only thing I owned after the war. It helped me forget, it made me happy again."

Chapter Five

CURRENT EVENTS

The old adage, *"Never say never,"* could pretty much summarize my life's journey, because everything I swore that I would never do as a teenager, I pretty much did as an adult! For instance, it's funny how I swore I would never go to a university or college near family, I ended up staying in Guam for school. I swore I would never get myself into debt, I got my first loan at 21 for a car that was way too expensive for me to be driving even at my current age. I swore that I would never be a teacher, I stayed in the education profession for over 15 years.

But in retrospect, the reason I entered my first career, immediately after graduating from college, was because a former elementary teacher called me one day and asked if I was interested in teaching 2nd grade at my alma mater, St. Francis School. Of course, I was flattered that she would consider me, as I always had a fondness for my childhood days at that school and I thought this was an ideal way for me to give back to my community for at least a few years while making some much needed dough as a college grad with some serious student-loan debt.

Thus began my days as an educator, and what I thought would be two years at the most, ended-up being well over ten. Working at the school was like working at home. My eldest sister Cathy was the music teacher and her husband Mark, the librarian, along with my sister Sophia, a Kindergarten teacher and last but certainly not least Natty was the development officer to help raise much needed funds for the rather humble and cash-strapped private school.

THE RAGDOLL and THE MARINE

It could very well have been renamed the Calvo Catholic School as we seemed to be everywhere in that institution of learning!

I became the type of Social Studies teacher that made it a point of having "Current Event Friday's"; even though, I rarely read the newspaper. Actually, I read the newspaper but only the pop culture, fashion and society columns. I figured everything else that was happening in the world of any importance, I could hear in a 30 second spot of news on the radio as I drove to school in the mornings or in the afternoons on my way home.

I'll admit that being consciously aware of what is happening in the world in which we live, is as crucial to education as learning about how to solve for X in math or about the dynamics of figurative language in reading. So, in my Social Studies classroom, I routinely had my middle school students read, write and present on issues and articles that they were faced with at the turn of the 21st Century from a newspaper. Like most typical educators, I sang the praises and spoke of the virtues of reading, reading and reading. The more and varied the reading you did as a pupil, the more you would benefit from the sheer knowledge, facts and details that you could regurgitate at a moment's notice. Actually, this little exercise in reporting significant news items for the week wasn't enough for me to catch the most important newspaper headline that would eventually change the course of Natty's life forever.

The person who had the good fortune of revealing that piece of information to her was my brother-in-law Mark. As the school librarian, he was always on top of any event happening in Guam. He read the entire newspaper everyday waiting for kids or classes to use the library. And unlike most stereotypical librarians, he was always composed and a little too laid-back. If a bomb exploded in the library, Mark would probably calmly sit in his chair, look up at the students and whisper, "Shhhh". So, on one particular day in February of 2001, Mark took his regular morning break in the student store on the campus. Natty was responsible for managing the store as part of her official duties and was busy stocking and taking inventory of the goods and supplies that were in high demand with the students.

He very nonchalantly asked, "Hey Grandma, you once told me a story about a toy that you received from one of the soldiers after the war, right?"

Without much thought about his question, she continued to inventory the snacks in the campus store and said, "That's correct Marky. Why do you ask, Son?"

"Well, have you seen the PDN this week? There's a marine liberator who's looking for the little girl he gave a rag doll to right after the war."

Natty dropped her clip board, stared him straight in the eye and screamed, "WHAT! That's me! I'm the little girl. Oh, my goodness, where's that newspaper? I need to read that article!"

At that very moment, I walked into the campus store and overheard Mark telling Natty about the news story. She was understandably excited about the possibility of actually meeting the soldier again after all these years as Mark and I frantically searched through the week's newspapers to find the article. Natty read the article out loud to us. It explained how this Marine Liberator was with a Historic War tour group that was traveling to the islands of the Pacific where the World War II campaign took place and how he hoped to reunite with a little girl that he gave a rag doll to after the Island was liberated. The article mentioned the name of the hotel that the gentleman was staying at, so I quickly dialed and asked the hotel operator to be connected to their guest Mr. Richard Washburn.

"There isn't anyone registered here by that name, Ma'am," the operator said.

"Please check again operator, he's with the Historic Military Tour Group", I pleaded as Natty sat near me, anxiously wringing her hands.

"Oh, I'm sorry but that tour group checked out of the hotel this morning. I believe they head back home today."

Chapter Six

THE SEARCH

Watching a beauty contest on T.V. like the Miss America or Miss Universe pageant always reassures those of us with more assets in the cerebral department, that when posed with a question like, "Whom do you admire and why?", that God does exist and fairly spreads out the brain and beauty gifts to each of us. Even though the most photogenic female in the competition may have a difficult time answering such a philosophical question, the average female would probably respond with any combination of the following: *I admire...*

THE RAGDOLL and THE MARINE

People who bravely overcome an obstacle in their life and come out better for it; Coaches or captains that rally their team to victory even when the odds are against them; The single parent who works tirelessly at two minimum wage jobs and puts their kid through college; The rags to riches businessperson who gives back to an impoverished community.

If ever I was faced with that question, without a doubt my answer would be Natty! After I hung the phone with the hotel operator, my admiration for my mother peaked at that very instant and it was singularly because of her ability to remain calm in spite of a highly calamitous and stressful situation. Let's face it, if I received the news that this soldier, who after 50 years tried to locate me, left Guam not more than a few hours before I attempted to contact him, I would be utterly devastated! But thankfully, Natty was the polar opposite of me and she was nothing but sheer grace under pressure.

I felt terribly guilty for missing the opportunity to have a heartrending story come full circle with a reunion for my mother and the gift-giving Marine. I blamed myself for not reading the newspaper in its entirety and thus losing the precious time for such a reunion to take place. I was frantic and completely useless as to what to do next. But Natty's tranquil nature and voice of reason made me stop panicking when she said, "Nicci, let's call the Pacific Daily News and speak with the reporter who did the interview with the soldier."

"Okay Mom, good idea, let's call the paper!" I said pacing back and forth with the cordless phone in hand. She looked at me, smiled and handed me the newspaper to ensure that we had the right reporter and phone number, again her every gesture and movement reassured and calmed me to the core.

Understandably, the reporter was apprehensive to give complete strangers information about this Marine Liberator in search of a particular little island girl and I'm sure that the excitement and nervous energy in my voice did not help to convince her either. Again, I was feeling defeated that I hit another stumbling block in making contact with the soldier, but in a moment of "Divine Inspiration", I simply handed the phone over to her and as only she could do, Natty spoke to her in a very maternal tone and told her story about the G.I. with a doll. Like a charm,s he relented and gave Natty the telephone number of a man named Richard Washburn from Lockeford, California. Finally, a name and a number, the very things we needed to make this story complete.

Guam has always coined the phrase: "Where America's Day Begins" as a result of the nearly 24 hour time difference between this tiny U.S Territory and the rest of the mainland United States. This further exacerbated the situation as we were forced to wait for almost a full-day to make contact with Mr. Washburn. It was approximately 2:00 Friday morning in Guam when we made the call to the California number at exactly 9 A.M. Thursday, Pacific Time. I was beside myself again but true to form, Natty was as unconcerned and fearless as a newborn baby on judgment day! This was the moment that she had waited for, almost all her life. She would finally speak with this stranger who gave her something in a span of five minutes that made such a lasting impression on her and I saw from her composure that she was ready to seize this opportunity.

We sat in the master bedroom of my childhood home that she and my father designed, built and lived in for nearly 25 years before his passing. Her phone was by a nightstand with a photo of my father and a candle that seemed to be perpetually burning near it. There were pictures of her children and grandchildren that seemed to encircle the entire space and the only other objects in her large bedroom were religious statues and crucifixes of every height, color and shape. It was fitting that we were surrounded by things and images that represented a life blessed with faith and family. She was indeed in her element and nothing in the world could make her less appreciative of her lifetime of good fortune surrounded by loved ones.

Not surprisingly Natty said, "Thank you Lord for giving me the chance to speak with this man who helped get me through such a terrible experience. Go ahead Nicci, call him now Baby!"

I put the phone on speaker so she could hear the initial conversation and dialed the number. The first ring startled me. It seemed unnaturally loud and long that I was afraid it would wake up the sleeping household. The beating of my heart grew just as loud as the ringing continued well over ten times, and fearing the worse, I put on a brave face to spare my mother from further disappointment. "Maybe, he's out of the house or still sleeping from jet-lag." I said matter-of-factly.

"You're probably right, let's try later", she said.

I hoped that our third attempt to contact him

would be the charm, but I prepared myself for "Three strikes and you're out". Persistently, I tried about an hour later and then at least every 30 minutes for well over five hours but still no answer, not even an answering machine to leave a message on. By this time, Natty was no longer always at my side each time I attempted to make the calls. It was like she just continued on her daily routine without so much as a worry of concern about our quest to contact this man.

"Mom, I'm still not getting through", I told her.

"Well, if God wants it to happen, he'll let it happen. Just be patient Nicci and don't give up hope."

Chapter Seven

3, 2, 1... CONTACT

I'm convinced that everyone on this green earth has a hidden talent or skill that is typically associated with something that a person would not readily share or divulge indiscriminately with an acquaintance. The reason is that the talent or skill in question is not necessarily worthy of bragging about or being proud of. Let's say for instance, my oldest brother, who shall remain nameless, could be flatulent on command! This skill could come in handy when you want to watch a certain TV show and need to clear out the living room to take control of the remote. More generally speaking, having Tourette's Syndrome that is linked with obscenities may not be considered a hidden talent, but when faced with an idiotic supervisor who is grating on your nerves, this will most certainly be an advantageous skill to possess. My mother could very well be diagnosed as legally deaf and most people would not dare say that being hearing impaired is a hidden talent, but my siblings and I would argue, that in the heat of an impassioned discussion about living within one's financial means, Natty would always use this disability to her advantage and feign that she could not hear us as we lecture her on the too generous an amount of almsgiving at our parish church. But, if we were speaking about a subject that was taboo in the same proximity as the discussion about monetary donations to the Church, she would miraculously hear every syllable uttered and call us out on it. Which leads me back to my point, that a hearing disability could be considered a hidden talent and in her unique case a double threat!

Subsequently, I too can boast of a skill that not many people will openly admit to possessing…I'm a darn good stalker or more politically appropriate a darn good investigative reporter or better yet a sleuth. As a general rule of thumb, I only stalk people for the betterment of the community and society at large; at least that's what I convince myself to believe. For instance, there was a certain school teacher who abandoned his position in the middle of the school year when semester grades were due. This abandonment of position forced me as an administrator of the school, to resort to my God-given talents and skills and locate this individual, as he repeatedly failed to return the numerous phone calls or emails I attempted to communicate to him. Luckily, I remembered that he lived in a certain apartment complex and so I called the manager of the apartments and verified that a Mr. Whatshisname lived on the premises in Apt. 205. Like a charm, the highly efficient property manager corrected me and gave me the right address. BINGO, we served him notice to get the records needed for course credits to be administered to students or be faced with legal action.

So, this stalker like quality came very handy when I was doggedly determined to make a connection with the man from Lockeford. Instinctively, I called the PDN reporter again. Maybe I wrote the wrong telephone number, thus the reason for the unanswered phone calls. Or perhaps, the reporter gave me the wrong phone number and what she thought was a number five was actually a six. Or maybe he left an address of some sort that we could send a correspondence to. I thought that somehow a simple error was made along the way and just asking for clarification would resolve the matter. Calling on my inner investigative reporter skills, I held on to the last strain of hope that I possessed in my being, as I explained to the reporter that my numerous attempts to contact Richard Washburn were unsuccessful. I told her that there was not even an answering machine on the other end whereby a message could be left. I'm sure that the reporter could hear the panic and frustration in my voice just like the previous phone call, when I about passed out from anxiety just trying to convince her that Natty was the girl who received the ragdoll.

When she finally had the chance to utter a response and told me that the Washburn's were perhaps still traveling around the Pacific as part of the historic war tour, I was completely relieved. She recalled that the Liberator mentioned that the tour group would head next to Iwo Jima before making their way back home. Logically, that explained the unanswered phone calls but I still had some doubts if I was in fact calling the correct telephone number and strangely enough I was flabbergasted at what the reporter said in the course of our conversation.

"You mentioned the Washburn's. Was he travelling with someone else?" I asked.

"Yes, he was with his wife." She said.

Why this little revelation struck me so oddly was that, for the first time, I realized that this man was an actual person, someone with a real life history that includes a wife and perhaps children and not just some fictional character from one of my Mom's tall-tales. This Liberator was a man who had a career, dreams, goals, ambitions and without a doubt also fears and difficulties in life. It was the mystery of the unknown that fueled my fire and curiosity. I needed to find him just like he felt the urge to comeback to Guam and find that little girl that he gave a doll to all those years ago. The enormity of this reunion of Natty Calvo and Richard Washburn would be pinnacle for both their lives and mine as well. Of this I was sure, and now more than ever I was resolute to make it happen.

"How can we confirm if we even have the right contact number?" I asked her.

THE RAGDOLL and THE MARINE

"Well, I think he left me an email too," she said.

"What? Oh my gosh, that's great!"

Chapter Eight

KINKS IN THE ROAD

Most people who are born and raised on tropical islands can describe in great detail the splendor of day's end in paradise. The balmy weather that normally remains about 80° throughout the year with the gentlest of breezes that move through the lush, green coconut palms as the surf hits the shore adding to Mother Nature's musical rhythm and cadence, finally culminates with hues of red, yellow and orange that sweep across the horizon as the glorious sun begins its decent in the vista. It can be heaven on earth, a way for Nature's beauty to be revealed for all to admire.

But, this picturesque utopia can turn on a dime and expose its dark-side with fiercely violent wind gusts of over 200 miles per hour, heavily laden sable clouds that refuse to let the sun's rays pierce through the darkened sky and brutally wild waves that reach skyscraper heights for well over 10 hours. In Guam, we call them super-typhoons and in 1997 one named Paka, plowed through the island and wreaked havoc on the old and fragile school building, the very place of my employment. The semi-concrete eighth grade classroom that I occupied as a home-room teacher was completely roofless as the tin pan-els that once covered it were strewn across the school campus like autumn leaves in a park. The devastation to the school was also reflected across the entire island, as electricity and water utility ser-vices were cut-off for nearly three months for island residents and many homes and buildings were left abandoned like bombed-out shelters from the ravages of war.

Although this natural disaster was significant for Guam, the frequency with which we experience these storms is so often that the tenacity and resiliency of island people are astounding. After these typhoons move away and dissipate in the vast Pacific Ocean and the sun shines brilliantly on our piece of paradise once again, the whole island community moves together and works like a well-oiled engine to assess the damages and begin the long and arduous task of cleaning and repairing. Everyone gets to work and pitches in - neighbor helps neighbor, family bonds are strengthened and living without modern conveniences makes all of us a little humbler and more grateful for the simple things in life.

Even though this typhoon happened four years before Richard and Natty's close encounter, by the time we made a connection with the gift-giving Marine; the students, faculty and staff of St. Francis School were still displaced. The entire school community had to relocate at least twice to temporary locations that were available, after the heavily damaged structure was deemed unsafe, in order to remain open until a new campus could be erected in its original school site. This was the primary reason Natty was hired to be the Development Officer at the parochial school; she took on the role of fundraising efforts to help cover the cost of a new school building. She was good at it and she did not let catastrophes, natural or man-made, get in her way. This resolve to get the job done no matter how long it took or how many set-backs were encountered along the road to recovery is what allowed Natty to focus her energies on the task at hand.

Shortly after the storm, she said, "God helps those who help themselves." Natty spoke as we were cleaning the ton of debris that was left from the super-typhoon in our yard and hand-washing clothes from rain water that was collected from huge drums that were strategically placed under roof gutters around the house. "What little suffering we are experiencing now, is nothing compared to the sacrifice Jesus made for us", Natty said.

It was second nature for Natty to make the most of any situation as she always saw a blessing in everything. So, even as we struggled to keep the school running in temporary locations and lost a good deal of enrollment, as parents withdrew their children, Natty saw opportunity.

"Maybe, Mr. Washburn will help us get funding to rebuild our school." Natty said as I became disgruntled and disheartened not just by the challenges we faced at the school in which we worked but now by the lack of progress in reaching out to Richard and his wife.

Natty's positive energy always re-fueled my fire and even though I was not a very savvy worldwide web user at the turn of the new century, which could have been another delay; thankfully, some of my family members were not as antiquated as I. So,

THE RAGDOLL and THE MARINE

with the help of my brother-in-law Jesse, married to my sister Sophia, the introductory email to the Washburns was sent through the internet. We left nothing to chance, covered all our bases and solicited the help of my Auntie Carmen, Natty's younger sister, the baby born the day before Guam's Liberation, to continue with the online and long-distance correspondences as it made for a convenient timeframe and more affordable phone call from San Jose, California to the Washburn's Northern California residence in Lockeford.

Auntie Carmen had been living in the Bay Area for well over 20 years at that time and the financial burden of oversees telephone calls could be another potential obstacle to getting Natty and Richard to physically meet each other, so having Carmen be Natty's spokesperson in California worked for everyone involved. As the Washburn's returned from their trip across the Pacific, the emails began to fly and excitement was palpable for Natty and our family as Carmen and Jesse updated my mother on a bi-monthly basis as to what was being communicated.

"You see, God makes things happen in His time, not ours," Natty said after Carmen told her that she and Richard spoke on the phone along with his wife Dorothy who was just as excited as he was to be speaking to Natty's sister in California.

"You just need to be patient because the good Lord always provides!"

Chapter Nine

THE GRASS IS GREENER

The accolades of a day in the life on a tropical island are numerous: the delightful weather year-round that requires nothing more than a pair of flip-flops, shorts, a tank top and sunglasses; the picturesque natural surroundings that become living, masterful pieces of art when looking out an office or bedroom window; the familiarity of the people that call and make the island home of whom more than half are somehow blood relatives of yours; and the convenience of living in an area within a small radius so that anything over a 30-minute car drive is considered long and cumbersome. These are but a few of the virtues of a tropical island subsistence.

Yet the reality of living in paradise, that is only 32 miles in length and 4 to 8 miles in width, can very well leave you feeling insignificant, insular and quarantined sometimes. The limitations are rigidly set and rather finite, that the only way to release the frustrations of knowing everyone you run into while you profusely sweat from the 99% humidity and swat mosquitoes that swarm around your very ex-posed skin, is to fly away, literally. Consequently, for most Islanders, the best cure for this type of "doom and gloom" is a trip to a big city: Hong Kong, Tokyo, San Francisco or New York City would do just fine. There is something to be said about the freedom of anonymity from living in an open and vast location with millions of people occupying it. Sometimes, you want to go where NOBODY knows your name and they don't really care that you came!

Ironically, just as things progressed in the corr-

THE RAGDOLL and THE MARINE

espondences between Richard and my mother's spokespeople and plans were made to have an actual re-union for the two of them; I was at a crossroads in my life. I was in my early 30's and going through a mid-life crisis about a decade ahead of schedule. I was questioning everything of worth or value in my career, my personal life and my mundane existence on a tiny island in the Pacific. I had been employed at St. Francis for nearly ten years; continued to live in my childhood home with my mother and recognized that my circle of friends was getting smaller. To make matters worse, I saw my contemporaries moving in forward directions, whereas I felt stuck. I felt isolated in a world that was suffocating me mentally and emotionally.

I desperately needed a change in scenery. So, in the spring of 2001, I took a very well deserved vacation to San Jose, California to visit with my two favorite relatives- Auntie Carmen and Uncle Ray. Ray was Natty's youngest brother who lived with their sister Carmen in the Bay Area. They were the "Cool" aunt and uncle that most of us wanted to hang-out with as they were definitely the single, hip, fashionable and social ones in the family. It was just what I needed to feel a sense of liberty and the quick, exciting pulse of the rat-race in the San Francisco Bay Area. Everywhere we went was so completely opposite of Guam that I felt exhilarated and embraced all the change and modernity I encountered. Even in the midst of the Dotcom Crash, I was living in a world that made every bone in my body pulse with an electricity that would course through my veins. I was in my element and for the first time, in a very long time, I felt alive.

My California vacation ended as quickly as it started and before I knew it, I was back in Guam, back to work, back to the same old routine. It felt like I had never gone on holiday but my only solace was that Carmen asked me to consider relocating to Silicon Valley. Her generous offer was to take me in for as long as I needed until I found a job and got situated, which I pondered very seriously. Weighing all my options and identifying the pros and cons, I had no doubt that the right decision for me was to move to San Jose, California. The only thing left to do was to seek Natty's consultation and consent.

"Mom, I wanna move to California and try to make a living out there. It's something I need to prove to myself I can do." I said to her without the slightest fear or doubt.

"If you've prayed on it and it's what your heart desires, then I give you my blessings Nicci," she said as she hugged and kissed me on the forehead.

This was one of the first major decisions in my life that I was absolutely certain in making, despite the fact that I was going out to California, without a job at the ready and leaving the only life I've ever known behind with my mother, siblings and best friends. I realized that starting this new chapter in my life would bring unforgettable memories, novel experiences and exhilarating encounters and I was completely ready for it! With my mother's seal of approval, I contacted Carmen and Ray and told them I would be packed up, moved out and headed their way by the end of June. It was a big adventure for me, I felt empowered, energized and self-assured that all would work out for the best, primarily because Natty supported me and with her love and prayers, nothing could go wrong.

"Think about it Mom, when I move out there I can help Auntie Carmen organize your meeting with the Washburns. At least now, one of your children will be involved in the plans and you know I'll always have your best interest at heart!" I told her this, as a way to make our eventual parting more palatable for me, more so than for her.

"That sounds wonderful", she said.

In spite of my eagerness to relocate, I played out the scene, of my being at the airport ready to depart from my life as I knew it, over and over again in my head. It always started and ended with crying, wailing and moaning, but nothing was further from the reality of it. Natty's reassurance, that the certainty in my decision was from the grace of God, made my departure from my childhood home, my island and most importantly my Mother easier to bear.

She saw me off at the airport with my bags checked in and my ticket and passport in hand. We stared at each other, embraced and with a gentle strength in her voice she said, "I love you my Darling. God is with you!"

Chapter Ten

LIFE AS WE KNOW IT

An event, situation or incident that can shape and change the world around you can be as innocent as a first kiss, as joyful as the birth of a child, as heartfelt as a marriage vow or as tragic as the death of a loved one. For me, making the move to California was such an event. The convenience of having my family close by was still very pertinent as I was living with Carmen and Ray. But in truth, this move was transformative and the feat of trying to eke out a life that I was forced to create and carve out on my own served as a formidable motivator.

THE RAGDOLL and THE MARINE

Even with the recent crash of the 21st century dot-com phenoms, I wasn't deterred from searching and hunting for work in whatever market would take me. I was doggedly determined that this is where I would make my mark and I was ready for all the hard work and pain it could involve.

Carmen and Ray were just as excited as I was to become their newest roommate; we immediately re-modeled the room that I would call mine, in the short term, and found great furniture pieces at a garage sale, that I insisted on paying for. It was my meager attempt at living on a shoe-string budget if I was going to survive in the "Concrete Jungle" of the San Francisco Bay Area. Albeit, shoe-string for the career woman that my aunt was, in the world of semi-conductors and high-tech companies, consisted of weekend shopping trips to San Francisco with a quick bite to eat and all things bubbly to sip at the Rotunda in Neiman Marcus on Union Square. I felt like I was the child that Carmen never had, and I thoroughly enjoyed how she showered me with experiences that made my life seem like an adult fairytale.

"Have you ever been to New York City?" Carmen asked.

"No, but I've always dreamed of going there. As a matter of fact, I've never travelled to the East Coast", I said.

"Well then, we'll just have to change that!" she said without so much as a blink of an eye.

Carmen insisted that I should take advantage of this new found freedom and enjoy a life that I would certainly not be experiencing once I did start working with the rest of the rat-race; so she advised me not to be concerned with finding a job right away. She and Ray encouraged and convinced me that we should travel as often and as far as we could, to make sure that I got a global perspective and an appreciation for world cultures. As for me, to have the world as a classroom setting, the masterpieces of art

THE RAGDOLL and THE MARINE

tangible objects within my reach and the residents of places that I had never visited become my fellow classmates, was a dream come true. I mean, who was I to object to this once in a lifetime opportunity?

My study- abroad first began right outside my back door with road trips all along the California Coast, from the majestic views of the Pacific Ocean on Highway One, to the mesmerizing fog that rolls in and encapsulates the Golden Gate Bridge. I was an over-achiever that wanted more from my two professors of art, culture and history. We ventured further east and took a short trip to New Orleans. The French Quarter became a little bit of an obsession with me. The intricate wrought iron corbels on the historic houses and buildings with the genteel beauty of Spanish moss and ferns hanging from practically every balcony made it seem like I could have very well been a vampire or Mayfair witch from an Anne Rice novel. Even though Uncle Ray warned me that we would smell Bourbon Street before we got to it, I was eager with anticipation and felt alive just watching the mass of humanity dancing, drinking, laughing and bead flashing while Jazz and the Blues made the humidity of the night more bearable.

New York City was next on our list of places to see. I knew that a life without travel was a sad life indeed and if the places we visited were that exciting and breathtaking, I could only imagine what I had in store when we'd finally get to the Big Apple, because if I could make it there, I could make it anywhere! The plan was to go sometime in the fall and I vowed that after Manhattan, I would seriously start looking for work.

Life was perfect; I was travelling with Carmen and Ray and we continued to make progress for the Richard and Natty Reunion in Guam. I even began to have a routine of sorts; I would wake-up in the week day and drop Auntie Carmen to the train station by 4:30 A.M. each morning, do some chores around the house and errands before heading out to do the usual 3 mile walk around the neighborhood then help prepare dinner with Uncle Ray and make the drive back to the train station to pick up Carmen by 4 each afternoon. It was a very charmed life and I was fortunate and blessed to be living it.

But life as we knew it and the routine of one day ended right after I dropped Carmen at the train station. I made it back to the house in San Jose and like normal, Uncle Ray was having coffee and making breakfast for the two of us. The difference that morning was that the phone began to ring at 5 A.M.

"I bet it's your Mom calling from Guam. Who else could it be this early in the morning?" Ray said.

"Hello...Hi Mom, how are you?"

"Nicci, turn on the T.V." she said in a rather rushed tone.

"What...why?"

"Something's happening in New York City. A plane just crashed into one of the Twin Towers."

Chapter Eleven

RESOLVE AND DETERMINATION

I t's often said that a person's true character is revealed during times of crisis: the quiet fortitude of Rosa Parks on that Montgomery bus, the captivating fervor of Martin Luther King, Jr. as he delivered his dream on the steps of the Lincoln Memorial or the tranquil resilience of Jackie Kennedy standing next to her husband's second-in-command while being sworn-in on Air Force One. These are well documented instances of heroic individuals in our history but imagine the courage and selflessness of the average person on the street, the innocent bystander who happened to be at the wrong place at the right time or the person who is not a First Responder but reacts immediately during a tragic event. This is who I thought about as Uncle Ray and I witnessed the second plane hit the Twin Tower on the live broadcast. At first I thought it was a story about special effects, but I knew from the fear in the voice of the reporter that what we were watching was real and in real-time.

My mind could not fathom such an appalling catastrophe, so I started to imagine all the men and women who were consoling, aiding and rescuing the victims of this unprecedented terror attack in the United States. I kept thinking about all the people near the Twin Towers that were helping the injured and I wondered how I would have reacted if I was in one of those buildings or on the streets of New York City. The fact that we sat and watched this tragedy unfold before our eyes made me yearn to return back to my little island in the Pacific that no one cared about or blamed for the ills of the world. I wanted to feel insignificant again, to go unnoticed so that nothing this abysmal would happen to me, my family, my people or my island.

But my cowardice was amplified when I spoke with my mother later that week and she reminded me that we too are a part of this great nation, the United States of America.

"Nicci, I wanna fly out to see Mr. Washburn in October." Natty said in a very direct manner.

"Mom, I don't think it's a good idea to be flying on an airplane at this time."

"Why not! Remember I lived through a war and those terrorists aren't going to scare or stop me from seeing and thanking a man who helped liberate our Island. I'm flying out there, because if anything, what they did in our Country only makes me more determined to show these evil people that America is the land of the brave and the home of the free! Tell my sister Carmen to book me a ticket right away!"

THE RAGDOLL and THE MARINE

In Guam, the Chamorro culture dictates that the elder sibling has a large amount of influence and power among the family members and much respect is given to them. So Carmen did as she was told and quite happily organized Natty's flight to the Mainland to finally make this long awaited reunion happen. This catapulted those of us in California to make Richard and Natty's first meeting as special as we could. Before Natty arrived to the Bay Area, Auntie Carmen arranged with the Washburns to drive from their home in Lockeford to San Jose for an afternoon bar-b-que at her house; Uncle Ray organized the menu, prepared most of the meal and decorated the house while I helped by cleaning and lending a hand wherever I needed to. The hospitality of the Chamorro is something that most guests or visitors recognize and avow to, so to welcome the stranger is to put your best foot forward and make him or her feel at home and important.

Waiting anxiously for Natty to arrive at the San

Francisco International Airport, I realized I missed my mother terribly and prayed that nothing tragic would happen. Again, true to form, Natty came out of the Arrivals area with a huge smile on her face and a beam of positive, loving energy that emanated from her. All my angst and tension melted immediately as I saw her coming toward me.

"Hafa Adai my family...I made it!" she said.

"Gosh Mama, you look great. How was the flight?" I asked.

"I practically had the whole plane to myself, I think there were only 20 people on it including the pilot and flight attendants. It was the smoothest ride I've ever been on."

The day of the reunion was the nicest Fall afternoon, without it being too cold or too wet. The house was immaculately kept already, but somehow the cleanliness of it, made this reunion as pure and innocent as the act of the giving was, that brought it together. The table linens were pressed and laid out,

THE RAGDOLL and THE MARINE

the buffet scape was arranged and decorated and the aroma from the food wafted through the air. Everything was set and under control, all that was missing now were the Washburns.

I was nervous for my mother and couldn't stay busy enough to keep me from looking at the clock every second as time went by slower than the last hour of work on a Friday afternoon. All the questions started swirling through my head again: *Would this Marine and Natty get along? Was he and his wife nice and friendly? What did he look like? Did he suffer from wartime disabilities?*

In my frenzied state, I watched my mother and her siblings interact with each other as they laughed, teased and reminisced about their childhood growing up in the village of Chalan Pago in Guam; and then in an instant heard Carmen break into song with "God Bless America". Her soprano voice filled the festive house and this calmed me straightaway. It couldn't have been a better way for me to relax and thank God for the blessings that he had surrounded my family with: the gift of my mother and her baby sister and brother, the gift of a Marine who helped to liberate my mother as a toddler, the gift of life, liberty and the pursuit of happiness in a country that I was a citizen of.

"I think they're here," Uncle Ray yelled from the front porch, smoking a cigarette.

"Thank you, my Father in Heaven for making this happen to us," Natty said as she held my hand and we walked out the door to greet our most welcomed guests.

Chapter Twelve

WAIT FOR IT

Disappointments in life can come from the hype and expectations that we set ourselves up for: a favorite book that becomes a Hollywood film just can't quite beat our creative imaginings, a hopeful romantic possibility turns out to be a blind date from hell, the perfect outfit that you got online for a bargain with all sales final looks about two sizes too small on you. It happens to the best of us and so we live and learn to not be so optimistic next time; we become jaded to spare ourselves from the frustration and letdown. But once in a great while, some things are just meant to be exactly what we envisioned and if we're fortunate enough, even better than we could ever imagine.

Such was the case with Natty and Richard's second meeting over 50 years later. Although we hoped for a reunion in Guam with all the fanfare and flourish that such an occasion deserved and with the potential for throngs of guests that would have been invited to such a gala; their meeting in San Jose was quite the opposite: charming, simple and private. This intimate gathering of Richard, Dorothy his wife, Natty, Carmen, Ray and me could not have been more perfect as every nuance and gesture could be observed, felt and appreciated.

As my mother and I walked toward the enormous, white, American made pick-up truck that had parked alongside the front lawn, I saw a distinguished, elderly gentleman with dark sunglasses, a tan polo shirt and a baseball cap in the passenger seat and then a matronly woman with blond, curly hair exit the driver's side and quickly approach the passenger door. They appeared to be in their mid-to- late 70's but seemed to possess a spirit and character that was fresh and youthful. She looked like the quintessential American grandmother with her patriotic attire and genial smile on her face but she acted and moved like a woman with a real robustness to her as she assisted him out of the truck and asked him to mind his step. It was evident to me by the way they interacted that these two people were in love with each other. It seemed that theirs was a young, blossoming love but ironically in their twilight years. She was gentle and affectionate and he seemed to bask in the attention that she gave him.

"Hafa Adai Richard and Dorothy! Welcome to our home!" Carmen said with such enthusiasm that took me by surprise. I had forgotten that she had been communicating with them on the telephone and by email and so the casualness of her voice was familiar to both of them.

"Hello, you must be Carmen," Dorothy said in a drawl that had such charm and affection.

"I recognize that beautiful voice," Richard said in a rather whispery and gravelly voice as Carmen proceeded to shake their hands and then hug each of them. He was a stately looking man and I could picture him in his hey-day with a Marine uniform on, standing over 6 feet tall at attention.

Natty was beaming with joy as she left my side and walked closer to Carmen while Ray and I stood in the background, to allow Carmen to make the proper introductions. I had the best vantage point to witness this momentous event finally take place, but my eyes began to glaze over and fill with moisture and before I knew it, Carmen said, "Richard and Dorothy this is my sister Natty, the little girl you gave the rag doll to!"

Richard turned to face my mother, placed his hands on either side of her cheeks and smiled. It was a long while before either one of them spoke as he methodically and very closely studied her face. "There's the smile that I remember all those years ago. You haven't lost it, it's still as big and beautiful today as it was the day I gave you that blond doll!"

Natty replied with a lump in her throat, "Hello Mr. Washburn, I'm so grateful to you for liberating me and my people in Guam. You changed my life!"

We continued to exchange pleasantries and introductions as Richard and Natty were standing side by side holding hands. All my initial anxieties disappeared as the naturalness and comfort of the conversation among us, felt like we had all known each other for years. A stranger to this crowd would never have guessed that we had all just met for the first time as the ease with which we connected to one another felt familiar and unassuming.

My first clue to the mysterious features of this doll was revealed when Richard mentioned that it was blond. I had always imagined a raggedy doll with black or brown hair, so I was anxious to know and learn more; but I knew that this was not yet the time to subject this Marine to a barrage of questions that I contemplated for decades. Dorothy seemed like a southern belle to me as she and Uncle Ray chatted about the selection of wine and cocktails that he had offered to her for refreshment from such a long drive south. Natty and Carmen were glued to Richard as he gentlemanly flirted with both of them while they playfully reciprocated.

Richard moved with the assistance of a walking stick that looked like it came straight out of J.R.R. Tolkien's pages from Middle earth. Which, in and of itself, is not uncommon for the elderly to use but it made him appear to be all the more wise, as if a modern day warlock or wizard. It gave him a bit more bravado and only then did a sheer slightness of movement emerge. It would have gone unnoticed if I missed it at the blink of my eyes, but as we entered the house with his dark-tinted sunglasses and his trusted staff at hand, he moved as if the stick led the way. It was the most peculiar intimation of something not quite right but as we settled in our chairs and began to relish in the company we kept, this oddity vanished.

I took on the role of bartender to the rest of the party, as I mixed and poured the drinks for our guests to enjoy; and happily did this simple task wanting to take in the conversation that was happening so quickly around me. I liked being the fly on the wall, observing and immersing in all the history that was unfolding before my very eyes. Carmen was indeed the gracious hostess as she effortless fluttered between Richard and Natty's nostalgic conversations about their wartime memory, and Dorothy and Ray talking about the verdant and lush house plants that Ray very greenly cared for. I could see how happy everyone was and I felt like we had instantly become a very close knit group even though I was quiet for the most part just marveling about how we finally arrived at this point and soaking every moment of it up like a sponge.

"Richard would you care for a cocktail or a non-alcoholic beverage?" I asked.

"Nicole come closer to me", he said.

I did like I was asked and stood beside him as he sat facing my mother. Then he motioned for me to bend down.

"Let me touch your face and see if you have the same smile as your Mama", he said.

That was it. His strange walk and eagerness to speak with people so closely was because he lost his vision. Finally, after 57 years, the little island girl and the Marine meet face-to-face and sadly, he was blind.

Chapter Thirteen

THE BLIND WILL SEE

H ave you ever wondered: if aliens live among us; if Lizzie Borden took an ax to give her mother 40 whacks; where Amelia Earhart and her plane landed; if the Loch Ness Monster exists; who Jack the Ripper was; if Bigfoot (Or Yeti or Sasquatch) is real? The list of mysteries of the world that many of us would love to get the answers for, can go on and on. What fascinates us are the possibilities or theories behind the unknown, yet just as cruel as never knowing the facts behind such historic secrets is the disappointment in discovering the truth. This was the dilemma I was faced with after meeting the Marine who gave Natty a toy. Was his story just as fascinating and poetic as the gesture of giving a child from a war-torn country a symbol of peace, joy and happiness or was it just a case of a standard issue toy that all the children were receiving after the war.

Like the opening of Pandora's Box, the opportunity presented itself to ask this man, who had been willing to sacrifice his very life for liberty for our people and country, all of my childhood questions and assumptions about my mother's very first doll. But whether it was appropriate or not to ask the myriad of queries I had about the circumstances leading up to the event was of concern. Worse yet was if I had to choose just one or two at the most to ask; this would be an even more agonizing decision to make. I struggled to find a way to broach the topic of the war toy as the conversations continued among those gathered in Carmen's house but like a kid in a candy store, I was dying to get a taste of that morsel of information and I wasn't quite sure how much I would have to pay for it. *What if the memory of the war was too painful a subject for him to reflect on? What if his recollection of the war and the events that led up to meeting my mother were somehow forgotten or erased? What if Richard Washburn just did not want to talk about it because there was nothing of relevance to discuss?*

Richard's physical blindness, which occurred a few years before their second fate-filled meeting, was not as dark and visionless as I was about his reaction to a request to discuss in detail that simple but profound gift giving affair. Thankfully my fears were quickly dismissed before I even dared to utter a word about the rag doll.

"That doll was a Christmas gift from my mother," Richard stated abruptly as if he was reading my mind as I stood near him.

He sat on the dining room chair in Carmen's house and began to eloquently and precisely relay how he, as a battle-ready World War II Marine, was in possession of a rag doll during the intense battles on the sandy beaches in Guam. He explained how his mother very cleverly sent a Christmas care package to her son who joined the 3rd Marine Division at Guadalcanal during the Pacific Campaign.

"I got word that my dad was in the hospital in Colorado, so I wrote to my mother and asked her to describe the nurses that were taking care of him," Richard said with a smile on his face.

"Well, she got me back by sending this Christmas gift and a poem that described every feature of that doll. Her belly was as plump as my mother's. Her eyes were blue like the gal that I was dating before I shipped out to war and her hair was as blond as the nurses that were taking care of my dad."

The visual I got from the description of the doll was priceless but even more invaluable was the look on Richard's face as he described how his mother sent this Christmas package which he received in the

THE RAGDOLL and THE MARINE

middle of July in of all places an island in the Pacific surrounded with enemy troops embedded deeply in the humid, dense jungles of Guam. He smiled and spoke softly with just the slightest crack in his voice while the orbs of his eyes filled with tears, but true to form as a Marine not one dropped onto his cheeks or face. His memory was as sharp as a tack and he spoke with such an ease in his heart that whatever horrors he witnessed and experienced, as one of the soldiers of the first infantry wave that landed on the Asan beachfront, this man-made peace with himself and his maker. There was complete silence after he told us about his mother as if a single, solitary sound from anyone or thing besides Richard talking would shatter that perfect recollection of his forever. We were all tense and literally at the edge of our seats waiting for more to be shared as he paused and looked up over our eyes that were fixed on him like heat seeking missiles. Even Dorothy, who more than likely heard his accounts numerous times, seemed as enthralled with Rich's storytelling as we were.

Richard's descriptions of the days of the initial battle to take over the beachfront and ridge from the Japanese forces were intriguing and thought-provoking and I knew that I was indeed privileged to be in front of this man who no doubt came from "The Greatest Generation" as he shared such profound moments of history with us. He described some of his close encounters with death in a way that was not braggadocios like one could expect from a proud Marine but rather in a solemn humility that came from the wisdom and respect of a human being who survived the cruelty and tragedy of war. The reality was that there was so much more to this man than just a bearer of a child's gift and I was guilty of pigeonholing him as just a soldier and making his selflessness so trivial.

"How did you manage to hold on to that doll without the other Marines seeing it and teasing you?" Carmen asked.

THE RAGDOLL and THE MARINE

His attention turned to Natty as he smiled and said, "I hid it under my pillows and well, I swore that I would give that rag doll to the first child I saw after all the fighting was done. So, thanks to my mom, little Natty came heading my way and the rest as they say is history!"

Chapter Fourteen

AMONG THE GREAT ONES

Generation Gaps are interesting to think about when as a Generation Xer, I still feel relatively young and hip compared with the Baby Boomers before me. But then, I realize that there are now two whole generations below me, Generation Y and Millennials, who think that video arcades were like the Speakeasies of the Roaring Twenty's or that Voldemort is twice as sinister as Darth Vader. These gaps widen when people talk about the accomplishments and successes of the contemporaries in their cohort, which normally corresponds with growing

THE RAGDOLL and THE MARINE

grayer, older and wiser. Thus, appropriately and rarely does success in life happen in one's twenty's. But for those whose age group was bequeathed, "The Greatest Generation", these accolades did not come in their twilight years but in their youth. They were the greatest not because they built something extraordinary or discovered an answer to a great unknown or became inexplicably wealthy as the creator of the mother of all inventions; they were the greatest because of their unselfish loyalty and sacrifice to their country. It was simply the right thing to do and they all did it, male and female alike.

As the afternoon sun faded into early dusk, all eyes and ears remained fixated on Richard while he continued to enthrall his audience with stories and tales of his life before, during and after the war. The story of a young cowboy who lost his first sweetheart named Dorothy as his country needed him. He looked toward his wife and explained how their youthful love affair abruptly ended in their home state of Colorado because of the 2nd World War when he enlisted in the United States Marine Corps and shipped out to join in the battles in the Pacific. Dorothy left her childhood home as well and moved to California where she too served her country just as nobly as he, while working in the ammunition factories as a "Rosie the Riveter". It would be many years, marriages, children and lifetimes later that the two would reunite and continue with their great love affair that was long overdue.

As I sat listening to Richard, it struck me that I was very fortunate to be in the presence of a man who lived during some of the most harrowing times in our world's history and he was a primary source, living, breathing and talking about it. The beauty of him speaking was that it did not feel like a lecture or a lesson or like I was forced to sit with a relative listening to their stories about life in olden times. This felt like I was a child again, listening to a great storyteller only this time it wasn't my mother. This time all the mysterious parts to the rag doll story would be revealed and I was captivated and entranced by it.

Richard moved very easily into his wartime experiences as he talked about an encounter he had during the battle to liberate Guam from the enemy forces. Knowing a thing or two about cattle and horses, this got him the edge on the other Marines in his division when they were in the middle of an intense shoot out in a remote and steep trench in the dense jungle on the island. Rich and his fellow Marines were on patrol as they swept the island for Japanese forces who hid in the natural environment of the tropical landscape after the initial battle to capture the beachfront in Asan ended. They waited and watched while surrounding a cave at the bottom of a ravine, where they were positive that the Japanese Army was taking cover. Suddenly, gunfire came from within the cave and before the Marines knew what was happening people were running from the mouth of the cave, up the steep cliff-sides. At first, the Marines returned fire until they realized that they were shooting at women that the Japanese soldiers used as human shields and decoys to distract the American soldiers.

"Hold your fire", Rich shouted to his men.

The women were too weak to run and Richard recognized that one of them was pregnant and appeared to be in labor. He quickly carried her off her feet and climbed up the cliff side to get her out of harm's way while his fellow marines assisted the other frightened women.

He said, "The sergeant in charge told me to stay with her as I was the only one that had any experience birthing another living creature. I did as I was told and when we made it back up the ridge, I placed her in the back of a jeep and helped her give birth to her little boy."

"Richard was she a local woman?" I asked.

"No, she was Korean. Unfortunately, the Japanese Army brought them to Guam during their occupation of the island."

The atrocities of the war in Guam also included some of our young local girls who were made to be "Comfort Women", a euphemism for sex slaves for the Japanese officers and soldiers. These war crimes were concealed by the Chamorro women that were forced to be in these brothels but their friends and families that witnessed such barbarism spoke the ugly truth without ever revealing the victims' true identity as a sign of respect for their privacy and human dignity.

"I was told later that she and her little boy were taken in the jeep and made it back to our main camp. I often think about what ever happened to that baby boy and his mama," Richard said with his eyes glossed over, but continued as if it was just a simple thing that he had to do, nothing unusual, just as common as brushing one's teeth in the morning.

After his company's mission on Guam was

completed, Rich moved on to the next big combat field in the Pacific, Iwo Jima. He spoke about the injury that he received while fighting there. It was a shot to his throat that caused the gravelly, whisper like voice that he now had and was the primary reason he was sent back home during the Pacific Campaign. Even after all the fighting that this Marine engaged in and all the heroic feats that he was directly responsible for, this journey back to the mainland on a huge naval hospital ship fascinated him as he became one of the first successful recipients of a whole blood transfusion donation from the American Red Cross. This unselfish act of giving one's blood for the benefit of a complete stranger riveted Richard and he made it his mission to one day pay a visit with the woman who made the generous donation that eventually saved his life.

Just as all Marines would, he kept his word and as quickly as he could recover from his war injuries in the Mainland, he headed to San Francisco seeking out the address of the woman who made the blood donation.

"I never did get to thank her in person for her unselfish act and bravery," he told us. "When I called her number that I got from the Red Cross, I was told that she died a while back before I was fully healed. In a small way, a part of her is still with me."

We all sat with a look of awe and wonder at this man who looked inexplicably ordinary but was so far from anything but extraordinary. His life would be the envy of most people and although in modern times we hear and see the Post Traumatic Stress Disorders that many of our veterans face when returning back to civilian life, for Richard, the goal was to work hard to keep his Country great. His postwar experience was a life that included a doctoral degree in entomology, a dedicated member of the Forestry Service for over 30 years, a published author in scientific journals and a proud father of two sons and a daughter.

Natty, Carmen, Ray and I were so mesmerized by his incredible life story that we did not see the time escape us. The darkness of night fell quickly upon us and we recognized that the long drive home for the Washburns would be tiring even for a teen-ager who just got a new car for his sixteenth birth-day. Knowing that the day would end, I shuttered to think that this would be the last time I would see this man and his beautiful wife who made every ef-fort to spend time with my family.

As we said our good byes, hugged tightly and wiped tears from our eyes, Richard faced Natty while making his way back into the front seat of their truck, and said, "Most people don't have the ability to be identified by a smile like yours can my dear. It took me many years and attempts to finally meet you again but as you know good things in life come with effort."

Chapter Fifteen

ALL GOOD THINGS...

E ver wonder what happens to famous people or soon-to-be famous people the day after a notable event or occasion occurs? For example, what does Meryl Streep do the day after she wins one of her multitudes of Academy Awards? Or, do President and Mrs. Obama have breakfast in bed the morning the oath of office is taken by the next Commander-in-Chief of the United States of America? Of course, a feeling every human being wants to experience is what happens to a Power Ball Winner the day after her lotto ticket numbers are publically announced? Granted, that "To Do" list must be long and exhaustive once you're declared the sole winner of the largest mega power ball in the history of the lottery. I digress, but my point is, when someone experiences, in an instant, the glory, excitement and joy of something extraordinary or pivotal- what happens after? Does one go straight down after experiencing the pinnacle or does a person bask in the glory of it all?

Interestingly enough, I was expecting to feel deflated or aloof, after Richard and Dorothy's momentous visit. But my disposition was far from being despondent; I was on Cloud 9 and was reveling in the auspiciousness of what just transpired. I believe the feeling was mutual amongst all of us; Carmen, Ray and Natty were more jovial and lovingly affectionate toward each other than I had ever witnessed before, and my mother and I seemed a tad bit closer if that was even possible. I know that some daughters tend to have a strained relationship with their mothers but that was certainly not the case for us. Somehow our bond was strengthened and I gather it was because we experienced something together that I don't believe Natty would have ever thought possible, meeting the rag doll soldier again. Life was good and we all relished in its magnificence!

I spent as much quality time with Natty as I could before she flew back to Guam. Despite, the wonderful visit with the Washburns and the magical time spent together in the Bay Area, I could see in my mom's eyes that she longed to be home; to her house that would be teeming with her grandchildren as they played hide and seek in the yard while she tended to her tropically lush garden under the clearest blue skies. I knew she was anxious to share with everyone the stories of her visit with Richard and Dorothy, and although I would be missing from the Calvo Clan, my mother was always happiest amongst her children and grandchildren. This fact comforted me as I was relieved and satisfied knowing that she would be returning to her perfect life in paradise.

As for me, my new life in California focused on the festivities of the upcoming holidays and enjoying the novelty of such an experience from what was the norm for me back home. Watching trick-or-treaters walk through the neighborhood on a cold and crisp autumn evening while hues of red and yellow leaves fell on sidewalks and roadways was so vastly different from Halloween in Guam where children were more likely to load up in the back of a pick-up truck, sweating profusely from wearing costumes on a humid and breezeless night while riding in these vehicles from village to village. Thanksgiving Day stateside meant watching football games on TV then eating a very traditional turkey meal with all the trimmings in the dining room. Where as in Guam, families usually gathered outdoors for barbeque chicken and ribs with a turkey as a side dish not necessarily the main entree. It was an anomaly of sorts for me and I was getting a kick out of comparing the differences and similarities of it all.

But the grandest of all the holidays soon came upon us, and as only Uncle Ray could do, the house was bedecked with decorations from top to bottom, ready for hosting the Season's soirees. It was my very first Christmas spent away from Guam and I thought that perhaps I would be just a little homesick. Consequently, I was waiting for a little jog of memory from hearing a traditional carol or looking at a nativity set that would hit me like a ton of bricks and rapidly start the waterworks, accompanied by wailing and moaning for my family and my mother; but such a moment never came. I was enjoying everything that was strangely new about this very traditional time of year and it distracted me from thinking of home.

Perhaps it was just me, but somehow in light of the horrors from how quickly our safety and security in our country was shattered in a single day, there was a real sense of unity and pride to be an American those few months after the September 11th tragedy. It made me take stock of what was important in my life in a very solemn way and although I knew that my dream of going to watch a show on Broadway or shopping at the Mecca of all retail stores, Bergdorf's, was likely not to happen anytime soon, I was blessed to be surrounded by a loving family and prayed earnestly for peace on Earth and goodwill toward men.

Then, one night while watching something on T.V. with Ray and Carmen, an ad came on with Mayor Rudy Giuliani. He was surrounded by New York City's First Responders and Broadway actors as he announced that New York was open for business and encouraged people to come and visit the greatest city in the world.

Carmen turned to us and said, "Ray, book our tickets! We're going to Manhattan. It'll be my Christmas gift to both of you."

THE RAGDOLL and THE MARINE

I couldn't believe my good fortune. I was so excited about going that I went immediately online searching for all things New York. Ray and Carmen were of course giving me advice and suggesting all the iconic places to visit and the typical New Yorker things to do and I could not wait for my next global lesson by the two greatest, most gracious, cultural professors ever. I wanted to pinch myself because my luck was coming in threes; first with my move to California, second with Natty meeting Richard and now with a dream trip to the Big Apple.

The prosperity of this first holiday season away from home was unbelievable and I was so caught up in the excitement of it that I almost forgot to call Natty to wish her a Merry Christmas and of course a happy birthday.

"Merry Christmas and Happy Birthday Mama! It's Nicci."

"Hi my darling! How are you doing," she said.

"I'm doing just fine. So, what've you been up

to?" I asked.

"Oh, nothing special. I had a physical yesterday with my doctor," she said.

"Really, well what did your Doctor say Mom?"

"Oh, it's probably nothing, but he felt a lump on my breast and wants to do a biopsy just in case," she said without any apprehension in her voice.

"Yeah, I'm sure it's just a subcutaneous cyst of some sort," I reassured her.

My new, found optimistic outlook in life really made me believe and feel strongly that everything was alright with Natty; all good things don't necessarily come to an end!

Chapter Sixteen

OUT OF SIGHT...

W hen things are good for me, I usually think that very soon, "The other shoe will drop" or that my luck will start to run out. I suspect that I may have inherited that trait from my father; as Natty was always the perennial optimist. The only other explanation for my "Doom and Gloom" out-look in life must be from growing up a practicing Catholic. My parochial education which taught me the basic tenants of the faith to include Reading, Writing and Arithmetic, also encompassed a healthy dose of guilt. It is especially pervasive when you're having too much fun in life and everything is coming up roses; something's just not right if everything's perfect.

Curiously enough, Natty's news about a biopsy somehow did not faze me. It was so out of my character to think that everything would turn out great and there was nothing to worry about, but that's exactly how I felt. This new-fangled life of mine caused a positivity and optimism that took root in my very core and I had complete faith that all was well and in order in the Nicole Calvo Universe. Mom would be fine!

The NYC vacation of a lifetime for this island girl meant that I was playing Frank Sinatra's "New York, New York", over and over again in my room as I listed all the places to see:

The Statue of Liberty, Ellis Island, Brooklyn Bridge, Empire State Building, Central Park, Times Square, Fifth Avenue, Grand Central Station, the Met, the Guggenheim, Rockefeller Center, Radio City Music Hall, Broad-

way, 42nd Street, Park Avenue, St. Patrick's Cathedral, Madison Square Garden, Wall Street, Soho, Chelsea, Lower and Upper Manhattan, TriBeCa, Chinatown, East Village, the New York Public Library, Ed Sullivan Theater, Columbus Circle, Chrysler Building, the Flatiron Building, The Waldorf, The Plaza, St. Regis, Saks 5th Avenue, Bloomingdales, Barneys and of course Bergdorf's .

I hadn't even included all the places to eat at yet like Carnegie Deli, Lombardi's and Sardi's; and then the lyrics hit me, "If I can make it there, I'll make it anywhere." But it took on new meaning with this expansive list, because really, how was I gonna "make it there" with only three days in the Big Apple. I knew I would never be able to "make it anywhere" with so many places to go and so little time to do it.

My apprehensions dissipated when I realized that I was going with Carmen and Ray. I didn't have to worry about it, I'd just go with the flow and follow their lead. As a matter of fact, Ray was coaching me with what outfits to bring and what not to do.

"Whatever you do, don't look up at the sky!" Ray said.

"Why?" I dared to ask.

"Because believe me, you don't want to look like a tourist. You want to blend-in with the native New Yorkers!"

If there's one thing you learn about Uncle Ray from living with him, he hates negative attention, so sticking out like a sore thumb was frowned upon and absolutely in the poorest of taste. He's not hip and trendy but classic and stylish. He isn't flamingly flamboyant but commands attention in a crowd like bees to honey. Most importantly he was well travelled and quite erudite. I felt like Eliza Doolittle to his Professor Higgins without the romantic twist, so I listened intently to everything he told me.

"There's an energy in New York City like no other place in the world," he said to me as we boarded the plane and took our seats. I knew that if

THE RAGDOLL and THE MARINE

Ray felt so strongly about this place then I was bound to have a great time and I couldn't wait to be there.

The flight from SFO to JFK was the quickest and smoothest flight ever but as the old adage goes, "Time flies when you're having fun!" We were all laughing up a storm and drinking Bloody Mary's on the plane and something prepared me to pace myself as I refused to pass-out from being drunk when we finally landed.

It was a beautiful President's Day weekend and I nearly pinched myself when Ray told the taxi driver to take us to Mid-Town Manhattan through the tunnel. This was it. I was finally here and instantly became bright eyed and bushy tailed as I saw the city's skyline in the distance. All the butterflies in my stomach almost came lurching out of my mouth from the excitement and anticipation. I couldn't wait to be walking the City's blocks or experiencing a New York Minute or having taxicab drivers honking and yelling profanities at the pedestrians who were too mesmerized with the metropolitan atmosphere that enveloped them. I wanted to experience the rudeness of a New Yorker who would snub the tourists from out of town and witness the notorious traffic jams in Times Square. I prepared myself to experience all the clichés that people who are not from Manhattan and her sister Boroughs have bequeathed on them and their residents.

As soon as the cab stopped, I looked at the cab driver waiting to hear him bark at us to get out of the car but this guy was nice and super friendly. He even helped us with our bags and gave us a tip that the diner on the corner of the block had some decent food and coffee. Perhaps, he was the exception. I'm sure my next encounter with a New York Native would not disappoint me.

More of the same from the bell hop and the front desk receptionist, but I explained this away with customer service and satisfaction, after all, they needed repeat patrons for their hospitality establishment. I knew that I had to be on the streets of New York to get down and dirty.

We went for our first sight-seeing tour and walked to Grand Central Station and true to form, I couldn't help but look up to see only the tops of buildings with just a strip of gray skies above.

"Stop looking up!" Uncle Ray whispered to me.

"I can't help it. I feel like an ant", I said.

"Ray, there's no one on the streets, have you noticed?" Carmen asked.

"I've noticed that even the traffic getting to Downtown was light. No one's here. It looks like the New York I've visited many times before but without the stampede of the masses," Ray said.

Our first day in New York was spent around Mid-Town. Later that evening, we headed toward Broadway to watch a play with dinner to follow at Sardis if we were lucky enough to get a table without reservations. It was nothing short of a miracle that we got tickets at Will Call to watch the Producers and then a table for three at Sardis after the show.

The next day, I committed myself to museums – the Guggenheim and the Metropolitan, while Carmen and Ray went their separate ways to go shopping up and down 5th Avenue. We planned to meet at Bergdorf's at the shoe saloon and I was happy to walk all 40 blocks from our hotel to the Guggenheim along Central Park on 5th Avenue. I acted like I had just as much right to be walking on the sidewalks of some of the chicest and most expensive real estate in the world and really no one even looked at me with contempt or disdain. The doormen were greeting me and some of the residents walking their dogs on the sidewalks even nodded in acknowledgement. I'm positive I walked passed a sunglass wearing, Gloria Vanderbilt in a Chanel suit. It was another beautiful day in the city and I was enjoying every moment of it tremendously.

THE RAGDOLL and THE MARINE

Our trip ended even faster than we arrived and all throughout our stay, Carmen and Ray kept telling me that this was not typical of the City. Everyone we encountered was genuinely nice and happy that we were tourists from California visiting for the weekend. I never did experience any rude or unfriendly New Yorkers, in fact, their hospitality and sweetness was what struck a chord with me more than the city's glorious architecture, world-class hotels, luxurious shopping meccas and exciting day and night life. It was the sincerity of the people of New York that made the biggest impression on me. They were their finest at their darkest hours and I fell madly in love with New York City and all her natives!

Upon returning home to San Jose, I knew that my eventual romps of leisure would have to end and I really wanted to look for a job and start a career that would make me independent again. There's something to be said about not relying on anyone and enjoying financial freedom. The strangest thought began to creep into my consciousness. *"If I started to work, how long would it be before I could take a trip back home to Guam and visit my family? How much money would I need to save to make this happen?"*

It was a brief momentary thought and I quickly forgot about it and started my earnest search for work in a very downtrodden economic slump. There were far more people than I with enviable professional and educational experiences in their vitae, who were forced out of a job because of the recent dot.com crash, but my upbeat outlook on life would not make me feel defeated at the get-go. I worked on my resume, applied to want ads in the San Francisco Chronicle and the San Jose Mercury, and sought the help of a professional head hunter to get me an advantage over others. Even Auntie Carmen circulated it to people she knew in the industry who may have had a vacancy to fill. I told her I wanted to do anything but teach again. This was my opportunity to change my career path and I was determined to do so.

Eventually, I had to face the hard fact that perhaps the only edge I had was my experience as an educator with administrative capabilities. I bit the bullet and started applying for teaching positions at nearby private, Catholic Schools. I convinced myself that one is more employable, when they're employed. Get the job and then look elsewhere while you're making some mula! It was my plan and I was sticking with it.

"Nicole, the phone's ringing. Can you answer it for me?" Uncle Ray yelled from the backyard as I was busy loading the washing machine.

"Hello..." I said.

"Nicole, it's Lea. I'm at the hospital, something's wrong with Mom."

I held my breath for almost a minute before I realized that my sister was still on the phone crying uncontrollably. This was it. The other shoe was dropping, my luck had finally run out.

Chapter Seventeen

A REVERSAL OF FORTUNE

Someone once asked me if I believed that a person could feel when they or a loved one would die; not every person, but those attuned to a sixth sense. Most of us would chuck it up to a mere coincidence or hindsight being 20/20 or even deja' vu. I certainly never experienced it when I lost my father at such a young age. There was never one inkling that he would die on that Sunday evening in March a week before his 45th birthday. But for some strange reason, the weeks and days leading up to my sister Lea's frightening phone call, made me recall discussions or thoughts that I had but with everything going very splendidly in my California residential transition, I don't know why such ridiculous notions would even surface.

There were little conversations and feelings that now upon reflection, should have signaled me to realize that my journey in life would take a drastic turn in direction. One such feeling was when I started to think about reasons to return back to Guam. This came to me in, of all places, Saks 5th Avenue in New York City as Uncle Ray and I were busy looking at a pair of Tod's that he wanted to purchase. Just out of the clear blue, it was absolutely random thoughts, "I'll go back to Guam: if one of my friends or family is getting married, for a family reunion, if I become romantically involved with someone and I want them to meet my family, etc."

The second was a conversation that Auntie Carmen and I had about regrets in life. She told me that if given a second chance she would still make the same choices in life to be a single, childless, career woman. That was completely refreshing to me as I knew that I was probably headed down that same path.

"But, my only and greatest regret is not going back to Guam to help take care of my mother before she died," Carmen said.

Her words struck me because Auntie Carmen was a woman who lived her life by her own rules. If you knew Carmen, you would know that one of her favorite songs is Sinatra's "I did it My Way" and she would sing it at the drop of a hat, out of the clear blue. Carmen would always tell me that she made many mistakes in her past but it was her decision to make and she stuck by it. She was certainly a woman of great substance and so hearing her admit to having a regret was a bit of a shocker for me.

How prophetic all of it was, as I fast forward to my standing with the telephone in my hand and Lea sobbing.

"Lea, I can't understand you. What's wrong? Where's Mom?"

"I took her for her biopsy at the hospital and her doctor said it was only going to be a needle biopsy that shouldn't take very long," Lea responded through her sniffling and panting.

"He just came out and told me that I have to make a decision right now."

"What is it?" I asked.

"I have to decide if he is going to remove her entire right breast or just close her up. He said the cancer is all the way up to her nipple. I don't know what to do. I can't reach any of those guys, that's why I called you," she continued.

As calmly as I could without yelling at her I said, "Lea tell him to remove her breast. Tell him to take out all the cancer."

"Nicole but she's under anesthesia. She had no idea that this was going to happen. What if she freaks out when she gets up and then blames me for allowing them to do that to her?"

"Lethia Marie, your Mother's life is more important than any body part. Trust me, she won't be angry with you. Tell him to remove it now!"

I spoke with such authority and a definitiveness in my voice that even I could not believe I was saying it. But I knew that everything I had just told my sister was right and for the best.

As soon as I hung the phone with Lea, I immediately ran to Uncle Ray and told him what was happening to my mother.

"What do you want to do Nicole?" he said.

Instantly, I knew that I had to call Carmen and ask her to loan me money to buy a one-way ticket on the earliest available flight back to Guam.

"Are you sure Nicci? Maybe you should wait until we find out what her prognosis is," Carmen said to me.

"Please Auntie Carmen, don't let me also regret not taking care of my mother."

There was complete silence on the phone and then she said, "Let me call my travel agent and book your flight home by tomorrow."

After I hung the phone with Carmen, I went into my bedroom, took out my rosary and knelt on the floor by my bed like I did as a child. My tears were pouring from my eyes like a running faucet and I prayed more fervently and contritely than I have ever done before. Each word that was uttered of the Hail Mary, the Our Father and the other prayers in the rosary was said as if discovering the power of these invocations for the first time. It was not just the rote process that was recited in the past but this time I meant each and every word. This time I was sincere. This time I was begging and pleading for God's healing powers. This time I was praying for my mother's life and I knew that she would be doing the exact same thing for us if the roles were reversed.

"Lea, it's Nicole. Pick me up at the airport tomorrow night at 6. I'm coming home."

Chapter Eighteen

LIFE'S LEMONS

There are things in life that one may despise doing immensely but musters on anyway for the greater good. Say for instance cleaning the bathroom, which is quite trivial in the grand scheme of things but is perhaps the least desirable chore of all time. Let's just say someone's gotta do it and leave it at that. A more palatable example may be physical exercise; cardio workouts, strength training, stretching and cross-fit are all necessary evils to maintain one's health. Some people may enjoy working-out but, I'm positive that I am not the only person in the world that exercises begrudgingly. Naturally, its companion would of course be eating a balanced diet: fruits, vegetables, whole grains and lean protein- recipes to live a life free of chronic illnesses. Of course, not everyone who exercises and eats a healthy meal is disgusted in doing so, but let's be honest the ideal would be eating all the pizza, pasta, steak and potatoes, doughnuts, ice cream, cookies and pies while binge watching your favorite series on TV and not put on a single pound. Alas, this will never be our reality, even if you're born with genes like Giselle or Kate Moss, but we all must eat sensibly and be physically active for the good of our health.

The least favorite thing in the world but a necessity in my life as an islander is flying on airplanes. This mode of transportation has always been a point of contention for me. I believe it started when I was quite young and remember flying from Guam to Taiwan with my parents on one of my father's business trips. It was a perfect storm of situations and conditions that heightened my dread of flying. The plane seemed to be closing in on me as the temperature inside the aircraft rose to a scorching heat. The noise level of the chatting Chinese passengers grew at least 10 decibels with every breath I took as we hit air pockets that rocked the aircraft back and forth. All I could do was stare at my mother for some sign of comfort, but instead of crying or talking, I spewed my guts out while holding the barf bag in my hand. It was not a pleasant sight or scent, so needless to say, I hate flying no matter how friendly the skies. Ironically my love for travelling to foreign destinations and exploring new cultures makes airplanes a necessary reluctance for my cultural and mental growth. Talk about Catch 22, and thankfully with age my flying atrocities slowed down but I still am a Dramamine addict and never leave home without at least two brand new bottles of the original strength packed in my hand carry.

Even with my less than favorable experiences each time I have flown on an airplane, the almost 24-hour flight from San Francisco to Guam, as I returned back home not knowing what state or condition my mother would be in when I arrived, was without incidence. *Was it because I did not focus on my insecurities and needs? Could it be my preoccupation with Natty's physical health? Or did I just overcome my motion sickness and anxiety of flying overnight?*

Instinctually, I told Lea not to tell anyone I was coming home. I did not want my siblings to try and talk me out of my very calm and rational decision to return home and take care of my mother. What I do know, without a shadow of a doubt, is that I never found a job in Silicon Valley for the 10 months or so that I lived there; I did not have a husband or have children that I needed to answer to or care for in California; and I had a duty to take care of my mother who now needed my help.

I walked out of baggage claims and saw Lea

standing in the arrivals lounge. Although I did not know how Natty faired after the operation, somehow with my praying for over 48 hours now, I was sure that God would give me the chance to see my mother alive if even for just a short while. We just looked at each other and embraced without uttering a word. I knew then that Mom survived the surgery.

"Do you want to go home to change or rest?" Lea asked.

"No, take me to the hospital. It's my turn to take care of Mom," I said.

As we drove to the hospital, Lea spoke about how afraid she was that our siblings would be upset with her for making a decision without waiting for their consultation but it all worked out in the end. No one was upset, no one objected to the decision she was forced to make on the spot. Everyone just gathered in mom's hospital room waiting for her to awaken from the procedure.

Then she said, "You were right, you know. She

woke up from the surgery in the recovery room and when I told her that the Doctor had to remove her entire breast. Mom just said, 'Thank you my Father in Heaven for making them take out the Cancer.'"

I imagined Natty's brilliant smile spread across her face as she said those words out loud to Lea and a tear fell on my cheek. With every ounce in her body and spirit, my mother always praised her Creator for everything in life, bad or good. She often said that when we are faced with challenges or sufferings in life, then God is even closer to us at our lowest moments. She definitely walked the talk and never faltered in her faith.

Lea explained that mom's doctor was sure that the radical mastectomy he performed got all of the cancer out but that she would probably need to get on some type of cancer pill regiment for about seven years without the need for chemotherapy or radiation. The news was just getting better and better and I was completely relieved to hear it.

THE RAGDOLL and THE MARINE

By the time we arrived, it was nearly the end of visiting hours for patients so we quickly rushed toward the elevator and walked briskly to her room. As we got closer, I could hear sounds of laughter from the hall and I knew that my mother would be making all her visitors feel absolutely welcome and making light of what could have been a very serious situation. It was mom's way of showing that nothing is impossible with God and laughter is the best medicine.

"Nicci, is that you my baby?" Mom said.

I stood at the doorway and just nodded my head. She was being visited by one of my closest friends Ben with his mother, Mrs. Diaz, my sister Sophie, her husband Jess and some of their children. In the span of 24 hours, her hospital room was filled with floral arrangements of well wishes from friends and family, "Get Well Soon" cards from her grandchildren hung on her wall and of course a crucifix and her rosary placed at her nightstand from her bedroom back home. The scene seemed like she was the visitor cheering up the patients and I did not want to interrupt the happiness that I was witnessing at this very moment. I did not want to shift the focus away from this woman who was lying in a hospital bed with a positivity that was radiating from her very core.

My heart filled with such raw emotions of gratitude, relief and joy and I felt the urge to just breakdown and cry, to run and hug her hard, to tell her that I was a selfish daughter for ever having left Guam in search for a more adventurous and exciting life. But, I stopped myself before I became a blubbering crybaby, held back these sensations and mustered the biggest smile I could emit.

"I heard there's a party happening here and I didn't want to miss it!" I said.

"Oh, my girl, what are you doing here? I'm sorry if you felt you had to come back because of me. I know you were having a great time out there in

THE RAGDOLL and THE MARINE

California. I don't want you to regret leaving and re-sent me for it," Natty said.

I felt a lump growing again in my throat. The sincerity in her voice and the fact that she felt that her present situation should not stop me from continuing with my so called "new" life, made me feel even more guilty. Her selflessness and concern for my feelings and welfare made me love her even more.

"What are you talking about? That's nonsense Mom. Look at the fun you're all having without me. I don't wanna miss out on any of it anymore!" I said.

The conversations and laughter continued as she told us that she always hated wearing a bra and so God must have heard her prayers by having at least one of them removed. Then she looked at Mrs. Diaz and said,

"Dorothy, we've had our babies and fed them with these breasts. We don't need them anymore anyway, right?!"

Mrs. Diaz chuckled and nodded in agreement and then an intercom announcement was made that visiting hours were about to end. Everyone made their way toward Natty to kiss her good night and I whispered to my sisters to go home and get some rest.

As I walked Ben and his mother out of the hospital room to see them off, he turned to me and said,

"You know what to do when Life throws us some lemons?"

"Yup, we make some darn good lemonade!" I said.

"And spike it with some top shelf vodka," he chuckled and held my hand tightly.

By the grace of God, I knew I was exactly where I needed to be, back home, with my family and friends, watching over my mother. This lemon was a necessity to make the best lemonade ever.

Chapter Nineteen

GREENER...WHEN WATERED

E ven in the most remote locations on earth, as long as human beings live and breathe, there's always going to be some half-truth or flat out lie that will be craftily assembled and relayed to the masses. Rumors are funny anecdotes in life that can have you either be a willing participant sharing in the discourse or an unwilling one, at the receiving end of it. It happens to the best of us, so I've learned that when you become the subject of water cooler gossip, just roll with it. Just take pride that other people would waste their precious time in spreading such incredibly imaginative scenarios about you; the juicier the gossip the longer your 15 minutes of fame.

It was the most bizarre thing, concerning my decision to very quickly move back to Guam, the word being circulated about my reasons for coming home so unexpectedly ran the gamut:

"Oh you, didn't know that she had an Ice addiction. Yeah, her family put her in rehab somewhere in Arizona but she didn't complete the 12 Step Program, that's why she's back."

"She went to California to marry some guy but he jilted her at the altar, so she came back."

Perhaps the most dramatic, "She was having an affair with a married man, got pregnant, left to the States, gave birth and had the baby adopted."

Perhaps the truth just wasn't that interesting to people – she's back home to help care for her mother who has breast cancer. Although I was flattered by all the attention to my drug induced love affairs, I had more pressing matters to contend with like helping to manage my mother's cancer treatment care and looking to become gainfully employed again.

The days and weeks following her mastectomy required more doctor visits with her surgeon, an on-cologist and her primary physician. I very willingly took on the responsibility of taking her to appoint-ments and the follow-ups, as I didn't have a job and had all the time in the world to get Mom back to top form.

It's interesting to watch breast cancer awareness commercials when a loved one is suffering from this disease. The word cancer survivor takes on a whole new meaning when it's your mother whom you're not quite sure if she is masking her suffering so that you don't worry about her painful reality, or if she's telling the truth - that she feels no discomfort at all. Her recovery from the mastectomy was quick and apparently painless as she never asked for her pre-scribed pain-killers.

"I wonder how my chickens are doing?" she said to me one morning.

"What? Your chickens? I don't know. Why do you ask?" I said.

"Because, I don't think you guys are feeding them the left-over rice from yesterday's dinner. I feed them rice every morning and they just come and keep me company around the yard while I'm raking."

"Oh, I see. Don't' worry, I'll scatter the rice for them today," I assured her.

"Why don't you go out for lunch or dinner with Donna, Ben and Glenda?" she said.

"My friends are just as busy as I am. Besides, I don't want you to be left alone," I responded.

"I'll be okay, I can manage on my own for a few hours," Natty replied.

It was an odd conversation, but I could see that the routine of taking care of my mother with her meals, medicinal regiments and general care, was making her irritable and uncomfortable having me around her all day long. She needed her space and her habits to resume without my butting into them and rearranging her daily rituals. I guess, it was the closest thing to being a married couple who both retire and begin to get annoyed with having the other around all the time.

Natty would never have told me to my face that she was fully recovered now and didn't need me anymore. Perhaps she felt a little guilty that she was the reason for my returning back home and now that her cancer was being managed effectively then there was no need for me to be around her all the time. The problem was I just didn't know what to do with myself or how to begin looking again for work in Guam.

There was never any regret on my part for the decision I made to return but I was, for the first time, at a loss as to what to do. I could go back to school to pursue a graduate degree; but in what? Or I could start to get the word out that I was looking for work among friends, family and former colleagues but I wasn't sure what I wanted to do. I was becoming my own worst nightmare, a visionless, jobless Gen Xer whose mother was getting sick of having her around.

Then one day, a close family friend came to visit Natty at our house and the conversations began to drift toward what my plans were now that Mom was recovering from her surgery and managing her cancer.

"Are you planning to go back to the States?" Delia asked.

It was the first time I became aware that I could actually go back and try once again to find a job in California but this time I didn't have the urge to relocate.

"Nope. I think I'm going to stay home and try to make a life for me out here," I said.

"Well, if you're still interested in teaching, I

think there are some positions that are open at the school I work at. I can put in a good word for you with the principal," she said.

"What school do you work at," I asked.

"Notre Dame High School. Didn't you graduate from high school there?" Delia said.

"Yeah, I did," I said.

God has a wicked sense of humor when it comes to the plans he has laid out for me. Just 10 months earlier, I abandoned my teaching career and was determined to carve out a name for myself in a new profession. I wanted to get away from teaching altogether but even the signs in California were directing me back to the classroom and not much was different in Guam. Here was an opportunity to stop irritating Natty with my constant badgering, get out of her way and start to earn some hard cash that I was desperately lacking. I would be crazy not to take advantage of it and so I asked Delia to make some inquiries on my behalf.

In less than a week, I – was called for an interview with the school principal who also happened to be an alumnae from the graduating class a year before me, was offered a position to teach Freshmen Literature and Senior Speech & Debate, received news from Natty's doctor that her cancer treatment did not require chemotherapy or radiation regiments and took my mother to her last appointment with her surgeon to remove her surgical staples. Everything was falling into place and I knew that in God's plan I was not done teaching just yet.

The funny thing about returning back home is that I started doing things that I didn't recognize I missed doing when I lived briefly in California. Blinded by the allure, majesty and fascination of my days on the Continent, I now realized I was missing a major component out there – my best friends.

Ben, Glenda, Donna and I were the "Fierce and Fearless Four". We did everything together before I made my move out West, and like best friends should, they all supported and encouraged me to make my California dreams come true. With my sudden and unexpected return home, they were just as supportive and understanding. We all knew that we would one day meet up and spend holidays with each other but I always envisioned them coming out to San Francisco while I showed them the sights and sounds of the city. With the three of them, I never laughed harder, ate greasier, drank heavier and talked easier than with anyone else in the world.

"Teaching high school students may not be as bad as it sounds, "Glenda said

"Yup, you never know, your future husband can be the divorced father of one of your students," Ben replied.

"Then you'd be an instant mother!" Donna added.

"Is that your pathetic way of making me see the bright side of things? Gees, with friends like you, who needs enemies," I said.

We all laughed out loud as if no one else existed in the restaurant. Somehow hanging out with them again made me confident I had everything I needed and wished for: incredible friends, generous relatives, supportive siblings and the world's greatest mother!

I was about to begin a new chapter in my life again, in a tropical paradise, where the grass is always greener and I was ready for it!

Chapter Twenty

THE PURSUIT OF HAPPINESS

S ome wise person once said that the company you keep, reveals volumes about you as an individual. So, thinking about how one chooses a friend can be exhaustive when you ponder how people come into your inner circle. For instance, some acquaintances are made because of shared commonalities, like your friend that's a patron of your gym or member of the church that you attend. Others can become friends due to proximity like co-workers or neighbors who over the course of your life you may lose contact with because of a move to a new career path or a lease on a new home elsewhere. Some people become friends by association; your friend is a friend of theirs and so naturally you may hit it off with your friend's friend. Then you have the besties that somehow make you a better person even when you feel like a lesser individual. These are the friends that are attached to you at the hip by a higher power. Friends, that even if you haven't seen each other for a long time, once you do meet up again, you feel like time has stood still and you get back into a rhythm with them that is simply unexplainable.

Naturally, Richard and Dorothy Washburn in the months and years that followed the reunion in California, increased the collective Calvo Clan as now both of them became a huge part of our lives, indeed, they were the friends that became family. They eventually travelled back to Guam and stayed in our family home on numerous occasions to include Guam's Liberation Day festivities. On one such visit, Richard walked the entire parade route on foot with his walking cane at his side under the hot, sweltering July sun. He was well in his eighties and nothing would stop this man from being right smack in the middle of such a celebration.

Even Natty's children and grandchildren began to call them Grandpa Rich and Grandma Dorothy. Likewise, Natty too would travel back to California and stay with them at their Lockeford residence for weeks at a time. On these visits to the Washburn's, the three of them would fly or drive to numerous Third Marine Division celebrations across the U.S., highlighting their story about the marine with the rag doll. Richard would call Natty, "Sis" and Natty would refer to him as "My Brother Rich" as they would make it a point to call each other each July 21st to commemorate not just the liberation of Guam but to strengthen their bond of friendship that became more resilient with each passing year.

It was this connection that Natty and Richard

developed and nurtured that made me aware that the greatest blessings in life are often times the little things that many of us overlook and take for granted: waking up and going for a morning walk, texting a friend to make plans for lunch, having your kid tell you that they need help with their homework, or preparing for a presentation at the office. In a very real way these things are also what connects us as human beings; our health, relations, family and career. No matter what nationality or ethnicity you claim, we all share certain fundamental values that make this world a smaller place to live in and make our human connection formidable.

My being a part, in a small way, of the second meeting between the marine and the little island girl made me take a more in-depth interest in the Pacific Campaign on my island that affected so many people and this spilled into my new job as a high school educator. I began to read with my freshmen classes about the war in Guam from what few accounts and books were written on the subject. The discussions that we had in my classes were lively as many of my students began to ask critical questions about their family's experiences in Guam before, during and after the war. As I taught my freshmen literature classes, my senior speech & debate classes started to discuss the United States' decision to engage in the Persian Gulf War. The debate topic was whether the United States should enter into a war to seek out weapons of mass destruction. By all accounts, the vast majority of the seniors felt that the U.S. had a moral duty to help citizens of the world that were being victimized by a dictatorship. One of the seniors enlisted in the U.S Marine Corps, ready to be sent off immediately after graduation for basic training to eventually be in the front lines as President Bush began the campaign in response to the September 11th Terror Attacks. I could not help but think of Rich as a young man enlisting to fight in World War II in the Pacific those many years ago, and I realized that my student enlisting for his country now was only possible because of an older generation's sacrifices for my people.

"Hey, Ms. Calvo, my Dad told me that Congress doesn't want to give Chamorros any type of payment for all the suffering during WWII. Is that true?" A student asked me in class one day.

"Yes, that's true Tim. Our representatives to Congress have tried numerous times to ask the U.S. Government to make some kind of restitution for the atrocities our people suffered but as we have no voting power in Congress, the legislation usually gets shot down," I said.

"That sucks! Then why do we continue to show allegiance to a country that treats us like second class citizens?"

As an educator, a telltale sign that your students are being critical thinkers from life's lessons and not just from those in a textbook is when you as the teacher learn from your pupils. I was aware that

since 1977, each of Guam's four Congressional dele-
gates drafted legislation to the House of Representatives asking for the United States Government to
pay restitution to the Chamorro people of Guam for
the atrocities suffered from the Japanese Imperial
Army during World War II. This legislation required the Congress to make this parity because the
U.S. Government forgave all reparation claims
against Japan with the signing of the Treaty of Peace
in 1951, ending World War II after the atomic bombing of Hiroshima and Nagasaki. This was to include
waiving any claims made by the citizens of all U.S.
Territories. But even with all this textbook
knowledge, I did not know what to say to my students who were now seeing how even the very basic
right to vote for a president that many of our Island's
sons and daughters have and will call "Commander-in-Chief" is something that people living
and born in Guam can never experience or participate in even though we are United States Citizens

from birth.

There were many times that I too questioned my patriotism to the United States of America when the issues of Loyalty Recognition Acts from Guam's delegate to the U.S. House of Representatives would get pushed aside on the session floor. Even in light of a War Claims Commission that determined from hundreds of written and oral testimonies of Chamorros who survived the war in their island, that the U.S. Federal Government had a responsibility to pay compensation for atrocities suffered during the war as a moral obligation not a legal one.

The big dilemma for me was, how will I continue to show the love and respect for Richard and all he and his fellow Marines did for my mother and our people who lived during those four harrowing years in Guam even in spite of how the right to vote for President of the United States, the right to have Guam's representative vote in Congress and the recognition of my people's sufferings for their beloved country, are denied for United States Citizens who live in Guam.

"Mom, do you feel that the Federal Government should give you money in recognition for all that you endured during the War in Guam?" I asked Natty one evening after a long, draining day at school.

She sat on a chair near the kitchen table and looked directly at me as if she too had been contemplating this very loaded question. Then in typical Natty fashion, she spoke with a simplistic eloquence, "You know what, many people died and suffered on both sides of that war. I'm grateful to God that my family and I survived it with the help of Richard and all those other men who fought so bravely for our liberty. That I will never take for granted. For me, the only compensation that is priceless and worth having is giving our people the right to vote for President of this great country that we call home. That will be all the compensation that I desire for myself and my heirs. That is my pursuit of happiness!"

THE RAGDOLL and THE MARINE

Chapter Twenty-One

A LESSON FROM A RAGDOLL AND
A MARINE

There's a crazy little thing called LOVE that some claim can be had at first sight or can be blind; can conquer all and will keep us together; or is a many splendored thing and can be endless. This four-letter word can also have different degrees of its existence. For instance, there's the love of a parent and child, a husband and wife, brothers and sisters, best friends, a neighbor, an animal lover, a lover of wine & spirits, a nature lover and even a motorcycle lover. Great thinkers have written poems, lyrics, novels and plays about it. Some have even conducted cross-sectional and longitudinal studies on it. It's been bequeathed as the greatest commandment under the heavens. It exists in every age, country and culture. Most would agree that life without love would be unsightly, hopeless and hostile.

So, when I think about how a little girl felt such love for a toy and a Marine, that are as different as ice cream and cactus, it made me realize that love also has no boundaries or limitations. The stereotypical differences between a rag doll and a soldier are so vast and great that their value and qualities are at opposite ends of the spectrum. Where one is soft, the other hard. One is used for playtime, the other at a time of war. One is huggable and cherished while the other's hardened and feared; a child's companion and a general's frontline. While one is always precious, the other always prepared. One is peaceful and the other is a peacekeeper; one is a security blanket the other maintains security.

THE RAGDOLL and THE MARINE

BUT, somehow their differences start to meld and intersect. The doll and the Marine can both promote hope in a world that yearns for it. They can each inspire admiration from the masses. Ironically, each can make it easier in life for the young and old alike.

So how does this cuddly object of a child's affection and this defender of a nation, play such a significant role in my life? That's simple, my mother. Natividad Rita Castro Calvo imbibes the very essence of both of these polar opposites. She has managed to maintain a balance of a gentle strength, a cautious courageousness, a fearless guardian and a peaceful warrior. As a child the stories that Mom told us fascinated me and helped to fuel my imagination and creativity about the world around me. The time she spent reading to us made me a lover of literature of every genre. Her devotion to her faith and belief in God, made me feel safe and secure that we were all being watched over and protected from

163

grave evil or danger. Her generosity and kindness to those in need and to strangers made me cognizant that life in service to your fellow man was the greatest legacy that one could aspire to. She lives by a simple but profound philosophy, "In life, always recognize the blessings and give thanks to God, no matter how difficult the struggle or challenge!"

Although Natty eventually loss her ragdoll, the feeling and memory that it evoked was so powerful and influential that somehow it allowed my mother to retain her youthful innocence in dealing with the joys and struggles as the matriarch of a family of 6 children, 19 grandchildren and 5 great grandchildren.

"Mom, did you ever think about what your life would have been like, if you and Grandma never ran into Rich and his platoon after the war?" I asked her as we sat around our kitchen table one summer afternoon on the eve of Guam's 72nd Liberation Day.

Her response was immediate. "No, I have never

thought of that. But what I do think about is that I never saw or had a toy like that before and once I received it, no other doll could compare – not a porcelain doll or a stuffed animal for that matter."

"Umm, you don't have to remind me of that. That's all we got as children remember or at least that's what we girls always got!" I said.

She laughed at me and then looked as though being teleported back to the exact moment she saw Richard kneeling next to her with a rag doll in his hand, those 72 years ago.

"I was just a small girl. So innocent at the end of a terrible war but growing up, I realized that the young man who gave me my first toy, although trained to fight and kill the enemy, had some sense of affection for a complete and total stranger. It was a symbol of love that he gave me and when we finally met again almost 57 years later – that love prevailed and grew stronger."

What she said that afternoon was an eye open-

-ing, earth shattering, time-standing still moment for me. For the greater part of my life, I focused on the rag doll. A tangible gift that unfortunately did not last very long, but was what I thought to be the most iconic thing in my mother's childhood. So for me, to finally discover at forty-something, with a career and independence that I am fiercely proud of, that I completely missed the greatest lesson in this story that I grew up hearing over and over again about a rag doll and a marine was humbling. Because really it could have been a stuffed monkey and an accountant; the item and the career are not significant. What does matter is that it was an act of kindness that eventually became a symbol of peace and love that had the greatest impact on my mother.

The mailed parcel that Rich received was given out of love; the love of a mother for a son whom she missed very much. This maternal love shaped him to become a man who wanted to serve, protect and defend a country that he loved. This man as a Marine, lovingly gave that doll to a young child who witnessed the terrors of war. And because of that one selfless act, the child felt loved and knew peace, which has made all the difference in my life.

Photo Gallery

Richard's Family

Mom, Dad, sister Sue and Richard
Taken when Richard first joined the service. He was 20
yrs. old.

Richard and Dorothy's 1st visit to Guam after the reunion with Natty

(1st Row L-R) Dorothy, Richard and Keiko - Natty's granddaughter, Mark - Natty's son, Mark Cruz -Natty's son-in-law
(2nd Row L-R) Ida, Natty, a family friend and Nicole
(3rd Row L-R) Jesse - Natty's son-in-law, Sophia, Skye, Forrest, and a family Friend.

Richard and Dorothy in San Diego, Ca.
before being shipped off to War

Richard and Dorothy in their Lockeford, Ca.
home - November 2015

L-R: Dorothy, Carmen and Richard in Lockeford,
Ca.- November 2015

Richard and Natty meeting after 50+ years in San
Jose, Ca. – 2001

Richard's College Graduation Photo

Natty's Family Portrait

Natty's mother seated with Carmen on her lap who was born the day before Guam was liberated July 21, 1944. Natty is the little girl to her mother's left, standing in front of one of her brothers. - circa 1947

About the Author

A native daughter of Guam in the Western Pacific, *Nicole A. Calvo* has devoted her life to perpetuating and preserving her Chamorro Heritage through her advocacy with non-profit cultural organizations. Writing has been more technical for her by way of grants, however, her love of literature spurred her to commit pen to paper and a series of poetry and short romance stories has thus been created.

The Ragdoll and the Marine, a Memoir, is her first book that captures a moment in her family history which showcased the kindness of strangers and ignited an enduring friendship.

www.nicolecalvo.com

91381255R00104

Made in the USA
Columbia, SC
16 March 2018